W9-BYK-360

COMES THE DARKNESS,

COMES THE LIGHT

COMES THE DARKNESS,
COMES THE LIGHT

A Memoir of Cutting, Healing, and Hope

Vanessa Vega

AMACOM

New York

Special discounts on bulk quantities of AMACOM books are available to corporations, professional associations, and other organizations. For details, contact Special Sales Department, AMACOM, a division of American Management Association, 1601 Broadway, New York, NY 10019.
Tel: 212-903-8316. Fax: 212-903-8083.
E-mail: specialsls@amanet.org
Website: www.amacombooks.org/go/specialsales
To view all AMACOM titles go to: www.amacombooks.org

Library of Congress Cataloging-in-Publication Data

Vega, Vanessa, 1971–
    Comes the darkness, comes the light : a memoir of cutting, healing, and hope / Vanessa Vega.
       p. cm.
  ISBN-10: 0-8144-7423-3 (pbk.)
  ISBN-13: 978-0-8144-7423-5 (pbk.)
    1. Vega, Vanessa, 1971—Health.   2. Self-mutilation—Patients—Biography.
3. Self-injurious behavior—Patients—Biography.   4. Psychotherapy.   I. Title.

RC569.5.S48V44   2007
616.85'820092—dc22
[B]

2006036161

Printing number

10 9 8 7 6 5 4 3 2 1

"You must carry the chaos within you in order to give birth to the dancing star." —FRIEDRICH NIETZSCHE

Acknowledgments

First, I give thanks to my Heavenly Father for showing me unequivocally that something positive can come from *all* things.

To all the health professionals who guided me on my journey. Today I stand taller because of the truths you helped me to discover.

To Dana Davis, my friend and mentor. You were the first to read these words and embrace them. Your honest feedback allowed me to search even deeper within myself for a truth I was afraid did not exist.

To my cohorts at the DFW Writer's Workshop, I say thank you. Your words of encouragement gave me the confidence I needed to see this dream through to the end.

To LP, I say thank you for proving beyond a shadow of a doubt that time and distance do not always mean the end of a friendship. After eighteen years apart, you welcomed me back into your life, learned more about the woman I'd become, and took this deep and personal part of me carefully in your hands without hesitation. Your kind words and reassurance gave me the confidence I needed to dig deeper into my past to reveal more of myself than I had originally intended. This book is stronger because of the questions you dared to ask. Bless you.

To my family and friends who have walked this long journey with me. Words cannot express how grateful I am for your presence in my life. No matter how many times I tried to pull away, each of you in turn reached out to me through phone calls, e-mails, and letters to let me know you were there for me no matter what. So many times I couldn't say thank you or express the love I have for you in my heart. I am so grateful to each of you for standing with me through some of the darkest days of my life. I am who I am, in part, because of your love and support.

To José, I say thank you for some of the most wonderful years of my life. Life has taken us in different directions, but I know that you stand with me in celebration of this endeavor. I wish you all the best, now and forever.

And finally, words cannot express the gratitude I have for my agent, Maryann Karinch, and my editor, Christina Parisi. For your unwavering support and endless patience, I am indebted. Each of you challenged me in ways I would have never anticipated and I am better for it. Thank you.

Dear Reader,

Of all the things I could have written about, this issue was by far the most personal and private. I have chosen to share my experiences with the hope that it will help you, the reader, to realize something greater about yourself.

What you hold in your hands is a culmination of more than fifteen years of therapy by many individuals at several locations. Some of this treatment was voluntary; some of it was not. Regardless, for the first time in my life, I was tasked with taking responsibility for my own behavior. To assist me in this process, I took antidepressants at various times of my life that offered me a small reprieve from feelings I found too overwhelming to deal with effectively. And in the end, I learned that therapy was about me and my desire for a healthier life. Period. It was not about my family, my husband (whom I divorced after twelve years of marriage), or impressing others. The false image I had created for the world crumbled as soon as I walked in the door. And as painful as that was, I am alive because of it.

When I entered therapy, seriously, of my own volition, and with a desire to get to the heart of the reasons for my self-injury, it was because I was cutting four times a day. I had tried, unsuccessfully, to break my own arms and femurs, although I *had* succeeded in breaking fingers and toes, and most recently, in rupturing the protective casing around my ulna and radius bones in my right arm. Repeated blunt trauma to my right wrist and forearm left me with temporary numbness in my fingers.

At the height of my disorder, in an effort to justify the endorphins I was getting from cutting, I subjected myself to medical experiments at the local medical school. I rationalized that if *I* wasn't doing the cutting, and it benefited society, then it wasn't really self-injury. I was donating plasma twice a week at the local blood bank and whole blood every two months. (In instances when I knew my weight wasn't going to be enough to qualify, I would purposefully line my pockets to tip the scale). Sometimes I would "drop by" the blood bank just to get my iron checked. A finger stick. A muscle biopsy. *Anything* to feel like I had control over the pain in my life. Anything to keep the pain from the past from catching up to me. Anything to keep from feeling like I was a phantom—a shadowy figure easily overlooked and discarded, forgotten.

My therapy was intensive and multilayered because I was also struggling with an eating disorder. To complicate things even further, repeated use of stimulants had damaged my body's ability to eliminate waste on its own. Deciding on a whim to stop the use of these stimulants turned out to be a near-fatal mistake. However, with medical intervention and medication, within six months I had retrained my body to function properly. I also discovered in therapy that if I focused on one disorder and managed to get it under control, the other would flare up.

I have never been able to fully maintain two disorders at the same time. Over the past fifteen years, cutting dominated my behavior and thought processes and anorexia was secondary. At times when my anorexia was the most severe and all consuming, cutting was in the background. It is like my body and mind can only focus on one thing at a time: feelings or weight. If I am obsessed with my weight, then it seems like I am able to shut off many of the feelings that contribute to self-injury. But if my eating disorder is under control, I start to fear getting fat, become even more insecure, and before I know it, I will go from cutting only once a month or so to cutting multiple times a week. This book is about my struggles to understand the causes for the manifestation of both disorders within me.

This is my story. I have tried to be as accurate as memory allows, although I have changed some of the names and personal details of the people included to protect their privacy. In some places, I have skipped over parts of my therapy because at the time it did not resonate with me. In the editing of this book, it was brought to my attention that I had failed to include a critical piece of information with regard to the group therapy format. From what I have written, one might get the impression that once the group was formed, we were thrust into our issues without there being an emotional safety net established. My omission of this step stems from the fact that I have no recollection of those earliest processes. In my mental state, I was not wholly convinced that I belonged in the group and therefore did not take any vested interest in its creation or duration. I clearly remember the first meeting and the intimidation I felt. But the subsequent meetings are a blur. Several weeks went by and as my condition continued to worsen, I began to realize that group was indeed something I needed. By then the rules had been created and the dynamics of the group were set. Although I don't remember the safety exercises created by the therapist, some part of my being must have felt secure enough to revisit the events of my past and to share openly my feelings about them. Now, I share them a second time to help you.

In the end, this is a story of forgiveness; redemption; and, ultimately, survival. I hope it validates what you feel or may be going through. I hope it encourages you to reach out and get help from someone who is able to look past the scars and tears and set you on a course to healing.

For now and for always, you are *never* alone. Know that in a world of billions, there is someone who can relate to and understand your pain.

With hope for healing,
Vanessa

COMES THE DARKNESS,
COMES THE LIGHT

The darkness started coming for me on Monday. Much like the flu, it hit the base of my spine first. The slight but undeniable tingling that just won't go away. I have a chill to my bones that I cannot seem to shake, even though I take two to three hot baths a day to try to alleviate it. My patience is nil. My sense of humor, gone. My desire to go anywhere or do anything has left me. I throw myself into a flurry of activity; if I run hard and fast enough, maybe I can beat it this time. Sometimes that works. But not this time. By Wednesday, the darkness is in my dreams. I am hurt. I am alone. I am dead. By Thursday I start to shake. I know what is going to happen and I feel powerless to fight it. I read a book. Flip through a magazine. Flip channels on the television. Anything to take my mind off what I know is to come. The darkness waits for me and I can't seem to escape. By Friday morning I have shut down. I am so far into myself that if I were to try to withdraw any more, I would implode.

At work, I can't seem to match the words coming out of my mouth with the voice in my head. People smile at me, look confused, and then walk away.

I am so tired. I don't want to do this. I desperately try to think of errands I have to do before I go home. There aren't any. Once I get home, I check the mail. Maybe there will be something inside that needs my immediate and undivided attention. Junk mail. As I walk in the door, I pray for a phone message, any message, any note or urgent plea for my help. Anything to save me from the darkness—to save me from myself. Usually there is at least one message. One voice saying, "Please call me back." But not today. Today, there is only the darkness, and it waits for me.

I take the dog out, feed him, slowly take off my clothes and get ready. The darkness has come and it's time.

Like all rituals, mine is exhaustive and demanding. Nothing can interfere with it or preempt it, or else it doesn't count. I don't want to have to do this again. I don't want to be interrupted, and so I walk into the bathroom and lock the door. Naked, I stand and take a long look at myself in the mirror. I look carefully at my eyes. I'm not there, but the darkness is. I look at my breasts. My thighs. My stomach. My face. And then I see my arms. They hang there, trembling. Waiting.

I hear a voice. Clear. Commanding. Unmistakable. It is my own voice, insecure and relentless.

You know you have to do this.

No, I don't.

Yes, you do. If you were better than this, you wouldn't be here.

I don't need to do this anymore.

Oh yes, you do. No one wants to hear your problems. No one cares that you're out of control. I mean, come on. If they did, wouldn't they have stopped this? It's Friday. Wouldn't they have noticed you haven't been yourself and asked you what was wrong? Maybe they would have asked you out for a drink after work. At the very least, they could have called. But they didn't, and so here we are. Don't make this harder than it is. You're a burden and people don't have time for this. Stop screwing around and just do it. I'm stronger than you are. I've been waiting for you all week. It's time.

The tears haven't started yet, but they will. I reach under the sink and carefully lay out my tools: cotton balls, alcohol, and scissors. I see a razor blade sitting on the counter, but I can't trust myself with it yet. Maybe I'm not that brave. Maybe the darkness won't see it.

I run my wrists and arms under the faucet. I use soap to make sure everything is clean. I have to. It's the rules. I reach for a towel and stop. Breathe. Close my eyes. Try, one last time, to fight the darkness. Now, the tears come. I open my eyes and look into the mirror.

All of my insecurities come out through a venomous inner dialogue. *I hate you. I hate you. I hate you. I hate you for being weak. I hate you for being too pathetic to be anything but what you are. I hate you for what you're about to do. I hate you for what you've already done.*

All of my failures come back in a rush. My eyes grow dark. *You're a shitty wife. A marginal teacher, at best. If you were as great as you think you are, don't you think you'd have received another teaching award last month? I mean, come on! And a model? Yeah, when's the last time anyone ever called you for a job? They haven't because they know you're fat and pathetic. So, now you think you can be a writer. If that were true, you'd be doing it, not just standing here thinking about it. And what do you really have to say, anyway? You think the world cares about your past? Your pain? Your ideas? Stop kidding yourself. If you were such a great communicator, or had a "great message," your book would be out by now. Face it. Nobody cares. You're a freak! You push away the people who love you the most. You can't communicate. You have nothing to offer. Give up. Give in. Stop jerking around and do this! Do what you know the best. Hurt. But you know you're going to screw this up, too. If you'd do it right, you'd cut out all of the parts of yourself that are unacceptable. But you can't, can you? You can't even do this right. Go on. Look at yourself. See how pathetic you really are. Naked. Crying. Ashamed. Is this what you were made for?*

Alcohol. Swab. Wipe.

Face it. You're a mistake. If God really wanted you to be doing something else, don't you think he'd find a way to stop this? He isn't. There's no one at the door. The phone isn't ringing. The dog isn't barking. It's just you. And the darkness.

I look carefully at the scissor blades. I make a mental note to buy new ones. Here again, par for the course, I've dropped the ball. I should have bought new scissors already. But no, now all I have are the old ones. Used. Defiled. Covered with old blood and shame.

It's time.

I look at my wrist and see the scars that I've put there over the last twenty years. I cry. I am living a lie. When I made my first cuts, I swore to myself they would be the last. That if I could just get over the hump, the need for scissors and razor blades and knives would be over. One day, I told myself, I would be in a better place.

Yeah, right.

I have to be careful where and how I cut. If I screw this up, I will end up in the ER, and then I'll be committed. Maybe I should be. Maybe I'm crazy and don't even know it.

I take the scissors in my left hand and hold my right arm stiff. The darkness surrounds me and I let it carry me away.

――――――――

Time stands still. I don't know how long I've been cutting. Part of me can see my arm, but there isn't any pain, and so I don't know if it's real. I see my right arm running the scissors under a stream of water and congealed bloody skin slides off the blade and lands in the sink as a slimy clump.

My arm has gone from white to pink to red. I want to stop, but then wonder if it's enough. If it's not, the darkness won't leave, and I will have to do this over again. So I keep going.

My heart races.

I can't see anything but tears. And blood. And scissors. I'm hot. I'm tired. But I have to keep going. I know the parts of me that I hate the most are just under the surface. I have to find them and destroy them.

I don't know why or when I stop. The scissors are lying on the countertop and I'm holding my arm to my chest. It burns, but I'm afraid to look at it. I don't want to see what I've done. But I do.

Pathetic.

I'm back in my body now. My arm stings and I panic. It's getting late. I have to clean up everything before anyone gets home. I frantically start the shower so if anyone comes home, that's where they'll think I am.

I clean the blades and hold them up to my eyes. I wonder why they hate me so much. Part of me hates them back for not doing a better job. One day, perhaps they'll kill me. But today is not that day.

The cotton balls are at the bottom of the trash can. The sink is rinsed out and clean. The scissors are clean and put away. There is nothing that can give me away.

Except my arm.

Except my wrist.

Except me.

Sometimes when I cut it is an almost orgasmic experience. There is a buildup and then a letdown.

Each scar represents a simultaneous joining of two parts of myself: the one known and accepted by the world and the other known only in darkness. Shame prevents me from allowing this darker side of myself to show. Condemnation would only add additional pain to this purposeful injury.

Some of my scars were satisfying. I made them and afterward felt release. Feelings previously repressed, without an outlet, rushed out of my body as quickly as the blood flowed. Given permission to vent, my soul is purged of its emotional toxins.

But not today.

The voice of my inner self remains mocking, belittling, venomous. The darkness hasn't retreated. It calls for me to do more, to be *truly* repentant. *Why did you stop when you know there is more to be done? Typical. You're great at starting things and a real disappointment with the follow-through. Focus! Focus! Focus!*

My husband will be home soon and I can't let him see what I've done.

A war wages within. I must keep going. The voice becomes louder.

But I can't do any more.

I'm exhausted.

I step into the shower and cradle my arm under the showerhead. I close my eyes and focus on the pain in my arm. If that's what I concentrate on, I won't be able to give any attention to the pain in my soul.

I know what I've done. I was there when I did it. No one will understand me. No one cares why I did it, only that I did it and it's weird. I mean, who in their right mind carves themselves up this way?

Again the voice. But this time the voice belongs to my father.

You're a loser, Vanessa. You're empty inside. If you were worried about being attractive to anyone before, you've cinched it now. Models aren't scarred the way you are. Models aren't fat. Models don't weigh 120 pounds. Teachers are supposed to be role models. What kind of a role model are you? Is this the way you'd want your kids to grow up? It's a sham. If people knew the truth, they'd run. And you think you want to try to get a new job? Fat chance. You'd better be thankful for the one you have. At least you've been there long enough for people to see that you do have some redeeming qualities. Wait until they find out the truth. What will they think about you then? One day everyone will know who you really are and your charade will be exposed. You act so confident, so sure of yourself. Other people want to be like you. How will you feel when they learn what kind of person you really are? Weak. Fat. Insecure. Truly disappointing.

Standing under the cascade of water from the showerhead, I look at what I've done. Time starts up again. I strain to hear the sounds of my husband coming through the front door. Over the din, an inner voice, *my* voice, takes over where my father's voice left off. *What are you going to say this week when someone asks about it? What kind of half-ass, bullshit excuse are you going to come up with to cover up the fact that you did this to yourself? Not only are you pathetic, but you are a liar, too. So much for integrity. It's a miracle your husband hasn't left you by now. How could he find anything about you attractive at all? Yeah, he says he's going out with friends or family, but would you blame him if he wasn't? I mean, if he's not getting it at home, should that mean he doesn't get it at all? You know if he leaves you, it's because you've forced him to do so.*

You suck as a wife. You don't cook enough. Clean enough. Have sex enough. I mean, what do you do? He would be better off without you. At least then he might be happy. Just because your life is in the shits doesn't mean his has to be. Is it his fault you are surrounded by darkness? Get over it. Run away. Give him a chance to find happiness. You're only bringing him down, so get out of the way. You know this makes you an even bigger loser. If you get a divorce, you are no longer successful in anything you've tried. People say there's no shame in divorce as long as you tried. Bullshit. Yes, there is. That's all my life is, shame. So, now what? Do you give in completely and run away? Do you stay and fight this and risk compromising someone else's happiness? Face it. You suck and people are just too nice to tell you the truth. You can't polish a turd, and goodness knows you've tried. You know what you have to do. Run. Be the bigger person. Do the right thing. Keep this sorrow to yourself. If you share it, you're only going to bring other people down.

Resigned, I know what I have to do.

I turn off the shower.

My skin is pink from the heat of the water. My arm stings and the cuts are covered in a thin, white film. Despite my best efforts, my body is trying to heal itself.

If only something would heal my heart.

I want to lie and tell myself that this will never happen again. But it's a lie. It *will* happen again. Maybe later today. Maybe tomorrow. But it has to happen. The darkness will not go away until I do.

"So, Vanessa, why don't you tell me why you're here today?"

I stare off into the distance and consider how to respond. How many lies do I have left in me?

I desperately try to think of a smart-ass answer, and I can't. I'm too tired. Too defeated. Too afraid of what an honest answer to this question might mean.

Well, I was told I needed to come see you.

"Who told you?"

My husband.

"Why would he do that?"

Well, it's been a long time since you and I have talked, and he thought I might need to talk to someone.

"Okay. So what's going on? What brings you in today?"

It's a long story. I mean, I feel like I have a million and one things going on and each of them by themselves aren't that big of a deal, but when you put them all together, I feel like I'm drowning.

I tug on my sleeves. The counselor's eyes catch it.

"You seem to be really uncomfortable, Vanessa. Do you not want to be here?"

It's a loaded question. If I say no, then I don't really want help and I'm wasting her time. If I say yes, then I might actually need to be here, which means I might be crazy.

Um, it's not that I don't want to be here; I just think there might be other people in the waiting room that need to see you more.

"Interesting. What if they were to tell me the same thing about you? What would you say?"

I don't know. Part of me might say they were right. The other part of me might deny it.

"Let's talk about the part of you that believes you need to be here.

Your husband told you to come and you did. Why would you do that if you didn't really think you needed to?"

Well, I told him I would and I need him to believe that I am doing everything I can to get well.

"What do you mean?"

Well, it's hard to explain. Especially to you. I think if you were to know why I was really here you would think I was crazy, and then you'd think less of me.

"I disagree. I am trained to be totally unbiased. What I personally think of you is irrelevant. I am here to help you. I am here to help you, as you put it, get well."

Well, you say that now because you don't know what I'm going to tell you. What if once I tell you what I do, you think I'm a really sick person? What if you think I'm crazy? I don't want to go into a hospital. I don't want to take a bunch of drugs. I just want to be normal.

"So who do you believe is normal?"

People who don't have to see counselors.

"What if *you* were the one who was normal? What if the other people weren't as strong as you and willing to help themselves? What would you think about yourself then?"

I would say you are trying to make me feel better, so I will confide in you.

"And what if I am?"

I stare at the hem on my sleeves.

Okay. You want to know why I'm here? I want to feel in control again. I want to understand why I think the way I do, and why I do some of the things I do. I want my husband not to feel like he's married to a crazy person. I want him to feel free to leave the house and not worry if I'll be dead when he comes back. I want to feel like I'm really inside my own body, not just looking at it from the outside. I want to wake up each morning excited to be alive instead of feeling this suffocating wave of anxiety wash over me. I want to feel like I'm a good person, and not a disappointment. I want to look at myself naked and accept my body for what it is instead of hating it for what it is not. I want to be able to look at a pair of scissors or a razor blade and not think of them as an escape mechanism. For once in my life, I want to be able to communicate what I'm feeling instead of allowing the scars I create on my body to say it for me.

My heart is racing. My soul feels naked and vulnerable. My eyes search out a point of focus and find one: a dying plant on an end table. A small part of me wants to laugh. How ironic, I think, that I am searching for a new life with someone who can't keep a plant alive. A distant voice crawls to the rim of my consciousness and tells me this is a mistake. Panicked it might be right, I want to leave. But all strength seems to have left my body.

I wait.

I want to look at the counselor's face, but I can't. I don't trust myself with what I might see there.

"That sounds like a tall order, Vanessa, but not an impossible one. I appreciate you trusting me enough to tell me honestly what you want out of our sessions. But I'm sure you realize that my role in this is merely that of a facilitator. You are the one who has all the answers; you just don't know it yet. If you agree to start coming to see me on a regular basis, then I need you to understand what I will be expecting you to do."

She pauses.

"Look at me, Vanessa. I want you to really hear what I'm telling you."

I can't raise my head.

"You don't need to feel ashamed, Vanessa. Although I can't go into any specific details, I can tell you that each one of my clients brings with her an artificial fear that the things she does are the most horrific or bizarre. It's like comparing apples and oranges. There is no comparison between any of my clients or their issues. Each person is unique in his or her background or disorder, but they are all the same in that they share a desire to heal themselves and overcome the things that hold them back from achieving their full potential. That's my job. Not to sit back and make a mental comparison between the things you do and say with those of another client. Am I shocked by the things you've told me? Not really. Although they are shocking to you, I can assure you there are other people in this world who think and do some of the things you do. You are not a freak. You are not crazy. But you do need some help in redirecting the messages you send yourself. I want to help you do that, but I can't until I know that we are on the same page. Look at me, Vanessa. You must know that the fact that you are sitting here right now is the first step in your recovery. Is it painful? Absolutely. Will it get harder and even more painful? Almost assuredly. But if you will see this thing through to the end, I know you will feel better about yourself, your situation, and the future. You want that, don't you?"

I nod.

The tears that I'd been holding in the corners of my eyes have now splashed down onto my sleeves.

I look up.

"Now. You mentioned letting your body speak for you. Can you show me what that means?"

I was afraid of this. To hear about it is one thing; to actually see it is something else.

Are you sure you want to see this? I mean, if you didn't think I was crazy before, you will now. I've told you that I cut myself. Isn't that enough? Do you have to see it to know that I'm telling you the truth?

"Vanessa, I need to see what you're doing to yourself. I need to see, as a medical professional, that your wounds are clean and properly taken care of. If you need medical attention, I need to know that."

I don't. I cleaned my cuts myself. I'm very clean and very careful.

"Vanessa, I believe you. But I need to know what we're dealing with here. Are we talking one or two cuts or ten? Do you need stitches? I have to know where you are right now, and the only way I will know that is if I can see your injuries. I'm not judging you; I am only trying to help you. Now go on, show me what you're talking about so I can see the level of injury we're dealing with."

I look at my sleeves and picture the wounds beneath them. I think of the feelings that forced me to put them there.

I breathe in.

I wait.

I look the counselor in the eyes and then close my own.

Do I really have to do this?

"Yes."

But what if you see my arms and decide I'm too far gone for you to help? What if there is no help for me? What if I really am crazy and don't know it yet?

"Vanessa. There are millions of people in the world who injure themselves. Some do it by cutting, stabbing, or burning themselves. It doesn't mean you're crazy. But it does mean you need some help, and I want to give that to you. Now before we can go any further, I need you to raise your sleeves for me. Go on. I promise not to scream or run out of the room in horror."

I smile.

I breathe in deeply and push my left sleeve up first.

That wrist isn't that bad. *It makes me sad to look at it.*

Well, there's one.

I look at her.

She closes her eyes and nods.

And, here's the other one.

I raise my right sleeve, gingerly moving it over the bandages I have there.

See? I told you they were clean.

"Vanessa, I need to see under your bandages. I have more, so you can replace them if you need to. Can you take those off for me?"

Great. I thought for sure I wouldn't have to go this far.

"Do you need some alcohol to loosen the adhesive?"

No.

I carefully work my nail under the edge of the bandage tape. Slowly, slowly, slowly, I work my nail around the whole perimeter of the bandage. It's stuck to my wounds in the middle. Whatever scab I have will rip off once I remove the bandage. I give it a pull. The clear juice that had seeped out of my cuts has started to flow again. My wrist looks angry and red. It pulsates with pressure and feels cold as air hits the exposed skin.

I think I need another bandage.

She goes to get one from her desk drawer.

"If you want to, you can go to the bathroom and wash it off."

No, thanks. I'll just wait until I get home.

Carefully, purposefully, I put the new bandage on my wrist. When I'm done, I pull both of my sleeves back down.

Well, there you are. So, now what?

"How many days have passed since you did this?"

Two.

"Have you ever cut bad enough to need stitches?"

Yes, but not this time.

"Was that on purpose or do you have control over how deep you cut?"

It depends on how angry I am. It's like my anger and the feelings are all-consuming. When I'm cutting I feel out of my body. It's like I am watching myself from afar. And then there are other times when I am not consciously aware of how many times I cut or how deeply I cut. Those are the most dangerous times for me. By the time the episode is over and I realize what I've done, it's too late. Sometimes, when I am able to keep a tighter reign over my emotions, I don't feel totally out of my body. It's like a conscious part of my being is still in touch enough to limit how much and how deeply I am cutting. I don't want to draw attention to myself, and the second I enter a hospital, I know I will be asked what happened. I hate having to explain where my cuts come from.

"In these instances where you've had to get medical attention, have you told the doctors the truth?"

No. I think quickly on my feet and can usually come up with a plausible reason that sounds authentic. I don't want to be labeled a suicide risk and so I lie.

My throat goes dry. This is the first time I have ever acknowledged that I have lied to the very people trying to help me. I feel like the illusion of control I have constructed has been shaken to the core of its foundation. As if playing a game of poker, I feel like I have exposed one of my tells. Now that my therapist knows I lie, she too will start to deconstruct the things I say for inconsistencies. I couldn't feel more vulnerable if I were sitting before her naked.

"If I were to ask you about the first time you hurt yourself, do you think you could remember?"

Yes.

"Do you want to tell me a little about that?"

The first time I can remember harming myself with blunt objects was in the fifth grade.

"Did something significant happen to you at this time?"

That was the year I got my own room.

"That's a pretty big deal for a girl of your age. Was your room a happy place for you?"

No.

I look at the floor. In my mind I can see my bedroom and all of its decorations. I should have pleasant memories of that room and I don't. How many times had I thought of jumping out my window? Hanging myself from the ledge? Jumping out onto the wood shed below envisioning myself impaled? Free at last from the never-ending disappointment that even at age nine my life had become.

"Why not?"

It seems like I spent a lot of time there either being punished by my parents or because I was punishing myself.

"What do you mean by punishing yourself?"

Through the years, I had learned through experience that feelings, unless joyful, were not allowed to be expressed. My mother believed that the house should be peaceful when my father came home, and so any sibling rivalry that existed between my brothers and me was ordered to a quick resolution. A bad day at school was no reason to be short with your own family. Peace, no matter what the price, was always the order of the day. Feelings know no time frame. By their very nature, they linger. For whatever it's worth, my feelings have always seemed to stretch on indefinitely, good or bad. Abounding joy was one thing. All-consuming anger was another. I can remember my mother saying, "If you can't be pleasant, then go to your room. When you are ready to join the family, you can come back." Nothing about the feeling or the events that contributed to that feeling were validated. The message? You really shouldn't feel that way.

"So you would go to your room?"

Yes. Seething with anger, once there, I would literally want to put my hand through a wall. A personal, inner voice of reason stayed my hand. But this one time, I can remember seeing a hairbrush on my dresser and picking it up. I remember how heavy it felt in my hand. Something in me snapped and my mother's voice, like a tape recorder, played over and over in my head. "If you can't be pleasant . . . if you can't be pleasant . . ." I took the hairbrush and hit myself as hard as I could on the top of my head. Stars flashed before my eyes. Still my mother's voice running over and over in my mind. I longed to shut it up. So I hit myself again. And again. And again. Within moments, my head hurt so badly, I could no longer hear my mother's voice. The red-hot anger I'd felt when I entered my room had been replaced with nausea and a pounding headache. But the connection between physical pain and the diminishment of emotional pain was made.

"That was an amazingly powerful connection for you to make, wasn't it? Weren't you afraid of your parents finding out what you were doing?"

Absolutely! In fact, even more than that, I was scared of myself! I couldn't believe that I had that much anger inside of me that would prompt me to act out that way. I knew at that moment I could never let anyone know about that side of myself. *Never.* I wasn't an angry person really, but I sure felt like one. And I was horrified at the things I'd done to myself. And to top it all off, part of me relished the pain because it was so strong, it made my feelings and the voices in my head go away.

"Did you worry about what effect hitting yourself in the head might have on your health?"

Sure. But I think part of me figured that if I could deal with my feelings without having them condemned by other people as being inappropriate, then whatever consequence I suffered was worth it. I didn't realize that a person could build up a tolerance to pain. I didn't know that over time I would need more and more pain to feel better.

As the months passed, I wondered if there was a way to still hit myself without being as forceful. The headboard of my bed was hard wood. I realized that if I banged my head repeatedly against the headboard, the pain was enough to make "inappropriate feelings" go away. I also learned it was enough to make me pass out. This really scared me. I can remember waking up on my bed with my light on in a position I didn't put myself in. I was on my stomach and when my eyes opened, my head was at a most unnatural angle. I was probably only out for a few seconds, but I'd lost that time. I had no idea what had happened between my hitting myself and waking up. I had never felt so out of control and realized I couldn't do that anymore. If my parents walked in and found me lying there like that, they would know something had happened and I'd really be in trouble.

But that understanding of the situation didn't change the fact that as the school year passed and my peers continued to make fun of me, the level of isolation I felt increased. I started keeping a journal as a way to vent, but it wasn't enough, and so I went back to hitting myself until I passed out (usually late at night when my parents were in the basement watching television) almost on a nightly basis.

Fearing brain damage, I resolved to try to find something else I could do that would end in the same result. That same year I started pulling the hair out of the top of my head. I worked hard at getting out the roots. If I pulled out enough of them, my scalp bled. But getting ready for church one day, my mother noticed I had a bald spot on the top of my head. She asked me if I'd been pulling out my hair. I lied and said no. She was on to me and I knew I had to find another way to let my feelings out.

Before the school year ended, I had learned to pull the toenails off my pinky toes. Red, raw, and bleeding, they would offer me something the other attempts at release had not—*days* of pain. With each step, I did penance for the feelings I had that I shouldn't and was reminded of the consequences.

"Well, I definitely think there are some things that you and I can talk about in the weeks to come that will help you deal with some things better. Does that sound like something you'd be interested in?"

I nod. My mouth feels like I've swallowed a cotton ball.

"Okay. Well, here's what I'd like for you to do. I want you to come and see me for an hour once a week privately, but then I would also like you to start coming to a group session twice a week. There are several other women in this group, and we will be talking about some things that I think are relevant to you."

My pulse starts to race. Great. Now I've been categorized with other people who have problems and need help. This can't happen. How can my secret remain a secret if I am expected to share it with strangers? I can't handle any more condemnation.

I don't know. I don't want to have to share my disorder with the world. You may not be able to judge me, but other people sure can.

"I think you're selling these other women short. They are in a similar situation to yours. They may not self-injure the way that you do, but they do engage in self-destructive behaviors. What I think you will find interesting is that you are each dealing with some of the same foundational issues."

Like what?

"Like poor self-esteem. Like depression. Like perfectionism."

Okay, so what if I do all of those things and they don't work?

"Then we'll try something else. Don't give up on yourself before you even get started. Really dedicate yourself to this. You said you wanted to get well, so here's one way in which you can help yourself do just that. I haven't asked you at all about your cutting. I haven't asked you about the feelings you had when you were doing it, or the feelings you had after. I haven't asked you about the ritual you go through when you cut, but I know you have one. Most self-injurers do. Instead I'm asking you to try this. You might get some things out of it that you aren't aware of yet."

Okay. So when do I start all of this?

"Tomorrow night."

Tomorrow night?

"Yes. Be here at 6 P.M. Dress casually, and bring a pencil. You'll have work to do and homework to complete once you leave."

6 P.M.?

"Yes. It's an hour and a half session. You'll meet the other women tomorrow night. It's the first session, so you don't need to worry that everyone already knows each other. They don't. You complete the group. After tomorrow night, there won't be any new additions or changes. I want you guys to bond as a group and feel comfortable enough to be honest with one another without having to worry about people coming in and out of the group."

Okay. I think I can do that.

"Good. The group and your sessions with me are part one of your treatment plan. Now, I have one other thing that I need you to do for me."

What?

"Well, I want you to try to not self-injure."

Um, okay.

"You don't sound too convinced."

Well, I think you're asking for mission impossible.

"Why is that?"

Well, it isn't like I plan to hurt myself. It just happens.

"I disagree. I think there are signals that indicate that you will cut. I want to try to make you aware of those signals."

I think we should take this one step at a time. I feel like you are asking me to get rid of the one constant in my life. If I can't cut, what do I do with the feelings that are stronger than my ability to express them? If you take that away from me, how do I know I can do the things you want me to do? What will I do with all of those feelings?

"We have to find you a new coping mechanism. It's going to take time. All I'm asking you to do is to *try* to not self-injure. Does that mean you will never cut again? Probably not. The reality is you've self-injured for so long that you've learned to use this as a coping strategy. If I were to tell you to stop cutting from this point on, you'd probably leave here and cut just because you could. I'm just asking you to be aware of your feelings and the things going on around you. Maybe you can start keeping a journal of the things that happen to you during the day. That way, if you do cut, you'll know what the last straw was, so to speak. Cutting isn't random. It's a last attempt, by you, to exhibit some control over events or situations that you find totally out of control."

You make it sound like I'm not strong enough to deal with life so I have to cut to cope.

"Not true. But what I *am* saying is that before we can deal with the cutting, we have to know the underlying issues around it. I need your help in that regard. I need to help you understand why it is that one thing might set you off today and not tomorrow. What's differ-ent? How does having your period affect your moods and your reactions to things? Do you cut more when you're tired? These are things I want to help you discover. If you know, for example, that being on your period means you are more likely to cut, then there may be a chemical connection."

Well I know the answer to that already. I know for a fact that I cut more when I am on my period. My temper is short, things seem to bother me more, and in order not to be curt or rude, I internalize my frustration and usually end up cutting more. It seems like after my period ends, I am more able to deal with things rationally. It's weird; it's like I can feel my blood pressure rising, my fuse growing short, and before I have any other signs of a cycle, I know that it's about that time. But I guess we'll deal with that later.

I exhale. Talking about this has left me feeling exhausted and cynical.

A silence fills the room.

I start to stand up.

Okay. I know what you want me to do. I will try not to cut. I'll come to see you and I'll be a part of your group. Is that all?

"No. But it's a start."

I sit back down again and run my fingers over my eyes.

How long will this take?

"That's up to you."

What do you mean? I don't have forever.

"No one does. But I really think if you give this 100 percent effort, you will see that you are stronger than you think you are, and that you have more control than you believe you have. Best-case scenario is you learn a lot about yourself, you are able to lessen your instance of self-injury, and you live a happier life."

So, what's the worst-case scenario?

"I never talk about worst-case scenarios."

Why not?

"Because I need you to focus on the positive. I need you to be optimistic about where you are and where you want to go."

Is that *really* realistic?

"What do you think?"

I don't think it is. I think I should know before I start what's the worst thing that could happen.

"What do you think is the worst thing that could happen?"

I might learn I'm crazy and have to be institutionalized. I might not find the answers to my questions. I might start cutting more. My husband might leave me. I might not have a happy life. I might die.

"It sounds like you have a lot to lose if you don't try this then."

Okay. You win.

"It's not about winning. *You* are the one who came to see me, remember?"

Yeah.

The room where the group meeting is held was formerly a storage closet. As a result, it is small, intimate, and totally without the amenities of a regular office. It has been freshly painted and carpeted. Air fresheners are in the outlets to mask the smell of paint, and the walls are covered with innocuous-looking "think positive" messages. The only light in the so-called room comes from a floor lamp set on its lowest setting. If I didn't know any better, I would think I was waiting for a massage. But there is no music or waterfalls in the background. Only a set of chairs set in a circle, so close there isn't much room to extend your legs in front of you.

When I walk in, three of the women are already seated. I size them up, wondering what sort of messed-up shit they are involved in to bring them into this group. They also look at me. One of them smiles. I smile back and then look away.

Part of me wants to believe I don't belong here, that it's a mistake. But then I feel my wrist and the pulsating throb that still beats there and know that I do belong right here.

Before too long, the therapist comes in and sits down. She asks if we have pencils and something to write on. We do. There is only one vacant seat, and everyone glances at it anxiously.

In the end, that seat would be occupied for only a couple sessions. The young woman who filled it suffered from a disorder greater than the group could accommodate, and she was relocated to another group. That left me and the three other women.

Nyla is a woman in her thirties who suffers from anorexia. She has been recently released from an out-of-state treatment program and is required to attend group sessions as part of her outpatient follow-up. Becca is an overweight secretary in her twenties who has been raped both as a child and as a teenager. She has isolated herself behind a wall of fat in an effort to protect herself from *further sexual abuse. Sarah is a college student who has also been raped as a child and is now engaged in a devastating cycle of unprotected sex. She has recently contracted an incurable sexually transmitted disease and is fighting to cope with the new life she has inadvertently created for herself.*

And then there is me.

"All right ladies, tonight we are going to talk about anger. I want you to take a few moments to write down your first memories involving anger. Who is there? What is going on? What is happening to you?"

We all look at each other and pale. The topic of anger is a hot button for each one of us, and none of us seems ready to deal with it.

Um, so what do you want to know? How old I was? What happened to me?

"Yes. Think back to your earliest memory where anger was a factor and write about it."

I don't have to think hard.

My father was a strict disciplinarian. He had very little patience for anything less than perfection, and his expectations of everyone, including himself, were more often than not almost impossible.

As the oldest, if something happened, it was my fault. If something wasn't done, it was my fault. But if I could make it seem like it wasn't my fault, then the punishment wasn't as bad. So as a child, I learned to lie very quickly.

My earliest memory of anger stems from an incident involving my younger brother and me. I was probably age 4 or 5 at the time, and he was probably 2½ or 3. I resented my brother. I resented the attention he got from my parents, and all of the attention he stole away from me. Before he was born, I was the golden child. But once he arrived, I was number two. I didn't understand why my parents weren't happy enough with just me. And so I started to do things to get him into trouble. I believed if my parents were mad at him often enough, they would decide he was more trouble than he was worth and send him back. Then, I would have my place back in the spotlight. Then, I would be loved again.

I tried lots of things. Getting on my knees and writing on the walls with my nondominant hand so that it would look like my brother had done it. I would tell him to do things that I knew were forbidden and then run and tell my mother what he was doing so he would get into trouble for it. Nothing worked. And so I came up with one final plan. In my childhood mind it was brilliant. I could not have been more wrong.

When my brother was old enough to move out of the crib and into a bunk bed, I moved up to the top bunk and he took the bottom. Once we were put to sleep, that was supposed to be it for the night. No more drinks of water or bedtime stories. Lights out meant alone time for my parents. It was sacred. Even in knowing this, I decided I had to secure my place as my parents' favorite. And so I would wait for about ten or fifteen minutes after we'd been put to bed and I'd start banging on the walls. As soon as my parents would come rushing in, I would feign sleep and listen as my brother was yanked from his slumber and spanked.

I hated that he was getting spanked with a belt over something I had done. Especially after I had been banging the wall for several days. In the end, my parents realized it wasn't my brother after all, but me who was making all the noise. One night, as I started to bang on the walls, my parents barged in and caught me red-handed—literally. It was then my turn to be yanked from the bed and spanked. Only my spanking wasn't like the spanking my brother had received. Oh no. This one was extra special.

My father believed in mental anxiety as a disciplinary technique. It wasn't enough to know you were going to get spanked. You had the job of choosing your beating tool. I can still remember the smell of my parents' closet and the intense leather smell on my father's side. All of his belts hung in one place. Black ones. Brown ones. Reversible ones. There were so many. It was hard to choose which one. Not that it mattered. But that was part of the torture. You knew your choice was irrelevant. It was an artificial sense of power given to a hapless victim.

Once I had chosen the belt, I had to wait. I had been closed in my parents' bedroom and left to wait for my father to come in. The seconds seemed like an eternity. I strained to hear every sound that passed through the closed door. Strained for a sound that would give my father away and allow my body to prepare for the inevitable. I held my breath and waited.

When my father came in, his stride was long and purposeful. He grabbed *the belt from my hands and bent it in half. He snapped it several times and the air broke with a cracking sound. It was time.*

"Roll down your panties and lie down."

No, Daddy, please! I'm so sorry! Please!

"Lie down!"

Please, Daddy! Please!

Whack!

NO! DADDY, I'M SORRY! PLEASE!

Whack!

I tried to block the hits with my hands. I clenched my butt cheeks to absorb some of the pain, but it didn't work.

Whack!

STOP, DADDY, PLEASE. I'M SORRY!

I was hysterical.

Somewhere between the second and third hit, I'd bitten my lower lip. Blood stains dotted the bedspread.

"Get up! What's wrong with you? Why would you do such a thing? Do you know how many spankings your brother got because of you? You disgust me! Get up! Go stand in the corner."

I could barely move.

Stunned, I made my way into the hallway and stood in the corner.

I don't know how much time passed. Maybe thirty minutes. Perhaps an hour. But I stood there and cried. I cried for what I'd done to my brother. I cried for myself and my stupid plan. And I cried for my parents, because I really believed that they deserved a better child than I.

At some point my silent crying turned to sniffling. I had no tissue, and I'd been ordered to stand in the corner. I stuck my tongue out and licked the snot as it fell from my nostrils. I couldn't see out of my eyes, I had cried so hard for so long. And I knew if I asked for a tissue I would get into more trouble, and so I did what I thought I had to do.

I wiped my nose on my pajama shirt.

When my dad finally came to get me, my shirt was wet and starting to crust.

"Donna. Come look at what your daughter has been doing!"

My mom came in. Her eyes too were red from crying.

"What?"

"Just look! Look at her shirt! Why would you do that, Vanessa? You know better than that. I can't believe what a disappointment you are. First you bang the walls to get your brother into trouble. Now you stand here and wipe shit all over your clothes. What do I have to do to you to get you to behave? You know you don't use your shirt as a Kleenex. Now your mother has to wash it."

My shirt was wrenched from my body.

"Now you go and get a T-shirt. And be quiet. I do not want you to wake up your brother. Now go on, get out of here. I can't stand to have you in my sight!"

"Okay, ladies. Let's talk about what you wrote. Vanessa, let's start with you. Why don't you give us the high points of what you wrote about."

So I did.

I could barely make it through without crying.

It's amazing that this event happened almost thirty years ago, yet I can still hear it and see it as if it were yesterday.

"So, your dad was the disciplinarian in your family."

Yes.

"Did your mother ever spank you?"

Well, if she did, it was something small like a fly swat to the back of the legs or something. Her big threat was to tell us that we were going to have to tell our father what we'd done when he got home. Then, *he* would deal with us.

"So you learned to fear your father pretty early in life."

Yes. I feared and hated my father. A big part of me believed he got a lot of pleasure out of seeing his children cry.

A sea of bobbing heads fills my periphery. I look up for affirmation that I am not the only one who has these feelings.

"Why is that?"

I don't know. I just know that spankings were a big deal. They had to be done bare bottomed and with a belt—that *you* chose. You wouldn't just get one smack or two. There were usually more than that, and sometimes they left welt marks that bled. It was unnecessary, and I hated him for it.

"You said your dad had a ritual for spanking you."

Yeah. It wasn't enough to just get the spanking. There was this whole drama with picking out the belt, waiting for him to come in, him telling you to pull your pants down and roll over. If you tried to block it with your hands, sometimes your hands were held up out of the way or you were told to lie Superman style on the bed. There was no explanation of why you were getting into trouble, and there was certainly no way you had a side to the story. It was his way only. That's it. No apologies. No "kiss and make up" afterward. No. You were told you were a disappointment and an embarrassment and then treated like a pariah. *Both* of my parents had a memory a mile long and they weren't quick to forgive and forget.

"So you felt like you were always having to make up for something?"

Absolutely. I knew my actions were always in the back of my parents' minds. And I believed the only way to make them forget the bad things I'd done was to continually be doing good things. That way, all of my good deeds would outweigh my mistakes.

"But isn't that a lot of pressure to put on yourself? You were only a kid."

Tell that to my parents. I was expected, from day one, to be a little adult. I had to act like one, talk like one, and jump through all the hoops that a show pony would. I was one of the few kids I knew whose parents would take them out to five-star restaurants or theatrical productions because I knew how to behave. Believe me. I *knew* how to behave. And my parents loved the attention that they received when they took their kids out and people complimented them. "Oh, your children are the best-behaved children we've ever seen." "Oh, your children are so polite. You must be so pleased." Right. My parents were master controllers. They could control my brothers and me with one look. One raised eyebrow. One shake of the head. One look of disappointment. It sucked, because I was always second-guessing myself. If I do this, will my parents be disappointed in me? What if I do that?

"Good. Now I want you to think about what you say to yourself when you self-injure. You talk to yourself, don't you?"

Embarrassed, I look at the floor. To say out loud the things I hear in my head will make me sound crazy for sure. I wait.

"Vanessa, go ahead. No one is judging you here."

I can't believe you want me to answer that in front of all these people.

"Don't worry about them. Their turn will come to be on the hot seat. Right now, we're talking about you. I want you to see something about yourself that I don't think you realize. Just follow me. . . ."

Looking up, I meet her gaze. I avoid looking at anyone else in the room.

Okay. Yeah, I talk to myself. I look myself in the eyes and say some of the same shit my dad said to me when I was getting spanked. I'm a disappointment. I'm an embarrassment. I'm stupid. I'm worthless. I can't stand to have you in my sight.

"Good. Now what do you do when you're saying all of these things?"

I don't want to say anything else.

I notice a small spider making its way across the floor. Unconsciously I move my feet a little from its path.

"Vanessa, don't shut down on me now. What do you do when you're saying all of these things?"

You know.

"No, I don't know. I need you to tell me."

Why? What difference does it make? It's messed up, okay? I'm messed up.

"No, you're not. But you *are* avoiding my question."

What was the question?

"You know what the question is. What are you doing?"

I'm cutting myself, okay? I'm trying to remove all of those parts of me that are unacceptable. I am doing what any other person would never do. I make myself bleed. I look at it. I sniff it. I lick it. I watch it clot on the blades of knives and scissors and I wait. I wait for the voices in my head that tell me I'm a bad person and a disappointment to stop. I wait for the hurting part of me to feel better. I want to disappear but then realize as long as I'm bleeding and taking breath, I can't.

I can't stop crying.

Someone passes me the tissue box. I look up, expecting looks of horror, and I see a room full of crying women.

I'm a freak, okay? You're not supposed to want to hurt yourself. And you're sure as hell not supposed to want to keep doing it. That's it. This is too painful. I have to leave.

I dig under my chair for my purse and car keys. I look at no one but can feel their eyes boring into the top of my head.

"Vanessa."

What?

My eyes narrow to slits. I never imagined sharing this part of myself with another person. I hate that I have allowed myself to become emotional and exposed so quickly. I feel like all the air has been sucked from the room. I'm sweating.

"Vanessa. I need you to think about one more thing, and then we'll go on to someone else. What do you feel before you start to cut? Think about this carefully. Are you happy? Sad? Overwhelmed? Depressed? What sets you off?"

I find my car keys and hold them in my lap.

Most of the time I'm angry. I have a high, a really high, tolerance for the little frustrations of life, but once that limit has been reached, I'm out of control. And you want to know the stupid part? It isn't a big thing that sets me off. I seem to handle major crises just fine. It's the little things that add up and lead to a breakdown. *These* are the things that steal every ounce of control I have in my life. Getting a flat tire in the rain. Putting your last three quarters in a vending machine and then losing them. Paying all of my bills, thinking I have money, and then realizing there is one straggler two days later. Spending ten minutes navigating a phone tree, finally speaking to a real person, being told they're transferring you to the "right" person, and then hearing the disconnected signal. Having a parent tell you how frustrated they are that you can't "fix" their child. In a word, it's the stupid things that send me over the edge. In and of themselves, these events are manageable. But things like this *never* come one at a time. It's like a barrage and I feel overwhelmed. I hit overload and my wires short out. I would be embarrassed if someone were to ask me what was wrong, because on the surface, these things are no big deal. No one would understand how something so small could piss me off so much. But it does! And when that happens, that's it! I can't yell. I can't beat up anything. And I need to. If I had a million dollars, I'd have a padded room in my house just so I could go in there sometimes and bounce around for a while. *At some point I'd dropped my keys and my hands are gesticulating wildly.* But I *don't* have one of those. So I do the next best thing. I beat up myself. Sometimes I hit things, and then other times I just cut. All I know is that I am *so* mad, I can't see straight. I want to rip someone's head off! I want to scream at the top of my lungs. I want to have some control, any control, over the shit that is happening in my life and so I take some. I take control in one of the few ways I know how. I hurt myself.

Finding my keys, I stand and move toward the door.

"Vanessa?"

I abruptly turn.

No! Now I really am out of here. I didn't know group would be this hard. I don't want to have to think about stuff like this anymore.

"Vanessa, sit down and wait a minute. You've had a breakthrough. Do you know that?"

Breakthrough? What kind of breakthrough? I've just told you that I use my body as a cutting board. What kind of breakthrough is that?

"Don't sell yourself short. Look at the pattern here. Your dad beat you when he was angry. You beat yourself when you are angry or feel out of control. Your dad had a ritual that he went through before he gave you a spanking. You go through a ritual before you hurt yourself. Your dad said lots of horrible, self-esteem-destroying things to you when you were getting a spanking and you too say lots of damaging things when you self-injure. You are perpetuating a pattern that you were introduced to as a child. You didn't create this; you only adopted it."

I feel completely exasperated. I want to leave but feel compelled to hear more.

I return to my seat. For the first time I look at the faces around me. I expected them to be closed. But they aren't. Eyes open, they seem expectant and reassuring. In my mind, I imagine them being relieved that this scenario is all about me and not about them. For the moment, their secrets are still their own.

I slump back down into my chair. Given half a chance, I would slide right off onto the floor.

But I'm not a kid anymore. Why would I continue to do something so self-destructive?

"Because it's what you know. Over the years, you made the connection between anger and physical pain. Now, we need to work on breaking that connection. I'm proud of you for being so honest here tonight."

Slowly the air returns to the room. For the first time in minutes, I can feel my heartbeat slow and my mind clear. A small glimmer of light appears in my subconscious. It never dawned on me that I might be replicating a pattern of injury shown to me as a child. What if this behavior wasn't something I was condemned to do for the rest of my life? What if I could learn to express my feelings in a way that didn't require a permanent mark? Might that be possible?

Like me, each of the women was given a chance to share what she had written. For me, their voices sounded like they were talking underwater. I saw lips moving and heard sounds but did not process one thing they said. My mind was elsewhere. I was trying to imagine a life without cutting. Five years in the future. Ten years in the future. Fifty years in the future. And no matter how hard I tried, I couldn't. Each time I tried to envision a scenario where I had strong feelings and wanted to be heard, I saw myself mute: voiceless and powerless against an urge stronger than any other I have ever known. And as I sat there, that small glimmer of light exploded into a million tiny shards.

I want to say something but realize it's too late. The session is over and everyone is collecting her things.

"Vanessa? Is there something you want to say?"

No. I was just thinking about something you said. We can talk about it later.

"Are you sure?"

Yes.

Nodding, I walk out the door. For me to admit that my glimmer of hope has already been extinguished would make me certifiably hopeless, and I need someone to believe I can get better, even if right now it isn't me.

In my dreams I am perfect. I am the one person everyone looks up to. In real life, if you were to ask most people who know me, they would probably tell you I am one of the most energetic and driven people they know. With that drive comes a certain level of accomplishment. I am the person who will put in more hours to be the best. I will go after the accolades most people don't want to waste their time on. I am the one who overcommits herself and as a result has earned the respect and praise of many people in the community where I live. I am an excellent role model to others and the go-to person for everyone else. The word no isn't in my vocabulary. My walls are littered with awards and com-mendations, and although I am the first to shrug them off, I take a deep, private pride in each and every one of them. For me, these awards validate that I am what I say I am, which is tenacious, professional, well educated, and generous with my time and resources. To the world, these awards represent a strength of both character and work ethic. Without them, there would be no proof that I even existed—that my life was one of meaning and accomplishment. With them, I have substance and worth.

I know where I get this attitude from. My father has already done more in his lifetime than most people will ever do. There are few places in the world he has not been, and few things he knows nothing about. He is by far the smartest and most driven person I know. For as long as I can remember, I have wanted to be just like him.

My earliest memories of my father are of him sitting at the kitchen table shrouded in a green cloud of cigar smoke. He was completing his PhD when I was born, and I can remember my mother typing out his notes on a manual typewriter while my father was at school and then redoing them later that night with new corrections. My father was like a god in our house. He was the provider and the only one who was allowed in "the study" (an enclosed sun porch at the front of the house). I can remember tiptoeing to the edge of the study and looking in. My eyes would wander across the room and fall upon stacks and stacks of papers and hardcover books. Fountain pens and their ink cartridges lay on the desktop and most prized of all, to me, were the yellow legal pads. How I longed to write on those pages! I saw how many my dad had filled and I dreamed of the day when I, too, would be important enough to write on paper like that.

When I was three years old, I decided to surprise my dad when he got home from work. I climbed up onto his desk chair with my purple crayon and wrote my "name" on the pages before me. I imagined how proud he would be of me! I would find out later that I had written on the final draft of his dissertation. But for that one moment, I wasn't a disappointment. In my mind's eye, I felt confident in the skills I had successfully demonstrated. I can feel the weight of that crayon in my small hand, chosen carefully out of a box of sixty-four colors. Even at three, my actions were calculated and purposeful. Sitting on my knees to reach the desktop, I pretended I was my father and vowed that one day I would be as important as I believed him to be.

"Tonight, we're going to talk about appearance versus reality. Everyone struggles with this in some form. That's why there are so many people with substance or alcohol abuse problems. Remember that. You guys are getting help with issues that most people have and are in denial about. So, my question for you this evening is, Who do *you* think you are compared to who others think you are? Got it? If they're the same, say so. But I think you would agree that they're not. That's what I want us to think about this evening. Are you ready? Write."

Great. Another chasm of emotion for me to plunge headlong into.

Breathe in and out.

In and out.

I don't want to do this.

I look casually up at the other women in the room. Only one of them is writing. Another has her legs up on the chair, knees up under her chin, and is rocking. Part of me visualizes her rocking right out of the chair and I suppress a smile. One of the women catches my look and looks back. I smile and quickly look away. I look at the door and wonder how many steps it would take for me to reach it. I don't remember it being that long coming in, but it looks like eternity going out. I think of my family, and how ashamed they would probably be if they knew I'd fallen so far. In my family, issues stayed in the family. To go outside that sacred circle was almost unheard of. That fact alone explained a great deal of the dysfunction that permeates my family tree. Okay. Enough procrastinating. Write.

I'm thirteen years old and my parents are less than a year away from being divorced. It is the summer before my freshman year, and I have made a promise to myself that by the time school starts again, I will no longer be an ugly duckling; I will be a swan. I haven't developed physically, and the comments about my braces, naturally curly hair, glasses, and lack of breasts have gone on for years. To my younger brothers, I'm "gorilla legs" and "thunder thighs." I'm 88 pounds of nothing but teen angst. I'm tired of crying. I'm tired of being made fun of. I'm tired of being unpopular. And so I go on a diet. At first, it was slow going. When I didn't eat my head hurt, I shook, and I was short-tempered. I thought for sure I'd have to give it up. But then I got the chicken pox and couldn't eat. It was the longest two weeks of my life. And the greatest two weeks of weight loss I could have ever asked for! By the time school started, I hadn't blossomed at all, but I had lost weight. I vowed that the bones I could feel would soon be bones I would see. I wanted to trace them with my fingertips and I believed that then, and only then, would I have the discipline I needed to be the perfect person the world seemed to expect. That summer was the beginning of the end for me. The end of the free and undisciplined Vanessa. My world and the way I saw myself in it would never be the same.

"All right ladies, I want us to go around like we did last time and share a little bit about what we wrote. I want you to connect what you wrote with the way you see yourself. I then want to know if the way you see yourself is the same as you believe other people see you. If it isn't, then I want us to see if we can find out why."

It's amazing how forgiving we are of other people. I sit back and listen to their stories and in my heart I offer my condolences. No one wants to be raped, and I can't bring myself to judge them for what they do to deal with that pain. When the issue of self-esteem comes up, I can't look at anyone in the room. How can I? I can't judge anyone for not having something I don't have either.

Sooner than I would have liked, it is my turn.

"Vanessa, you sure have been quiet tonight. Why don't you share what you wrote about?"

And so I did.

Who do I think I am? I don't know. I know who I try to be, and I know I've been unsuccessful in my quest to make everyone happy.

"Why would you want to make everyone happy?"

Because that's who I am. I don't want anyone to be disappointed in me.

"Why does their opinion matter if you're trying your best and are happy?"

Because I'm usually not happy. How do I know I'm *really* trying my best? How do I know that other people aren't looking at me, at my decisions, and thinking, "God, what a waste!"? I want people to respect me and think I'm wonderful. How can they do that if they aren't happy with me?

"It sounds like other people's opinions of you are very important."

Sometimes. I guess it depends on who it is. Some people matter more to me than others.

"Okay. Let's focus on the people who are important to you. What do you think they think of you?"

I think they believe I have my act together. They see me as someone who is a good leader and who is ready to do whatever is necessary to get a job done. I present myself as being confident, assertive, and totally with it. But it's a lie.

"Why is it a lie?"

Because I'm *not* confident. I *don't* have any self-esteem, and most of my assertiveness is a cover-up for my own insecurities. I want to be the best, and the only way I know how to do that is to work really hard and never give up. Sometimes, the things I put all of my energies into aren't the same things that other people would find important.

"Like what?"

Like writing or going back to college to get another degree when I can already get a job with the one I have.

"So what do you do when you feel you are a disappointment to others?"

I try even harder to make them love me. I get more awards. I accomplish something most people wouldn't even think twice about doing. I win them over with my deeds. Not who I am.

"And why is that a problem?"

Because what happens when I can't accomplish everything I want to? Does that mean I am worthless? Or worse yet, what if I've accomplished those things by mistake? What if I wasn't really the person who was the most qualified but rather the hardest to say no to? What if I'm not as great as everyone seems to think I am?

"Do you feel invisible?"

All the time. Every day. I don't know who I am. I really feel like if I wasn't always out trying to do amazing things, then no one would even know who I was. I would fade into the background. I would become my greatest fear—a nobody.

"So what do you do to make sure you haven't disappeared?"

I am always doing something. If I'm busy, then I can't disappear. I can't enjoy anything because I feel like who I am is connected with what I'm doing. If I'm reading a book, then I'd better have laundry going on at the same time. If I'm fixing dinner, then I'd better be returning phone calls at the same time. Always busy, busy, busy. If I'm busy, then I'm alive.

"What else? You can't be busy twenty-four/seven."

No, but I try.

Sometimes I feel dead. I retreat so far into myself that it seems like nothing or no one can get me out. I don't talk to anyone; I don't smile at anyone. I am just there. People look at me and say, "Wow, she's really focused." If only they knew how wrong they were! When I feel like I've disappeared the most, I have to have reassurance that I'm still here, that I haven't died and just don't know it yet. When I cut, I know I'm real. I can see proof that I am still here. I can touch my blood, feel it pulsate out of me, and know that Vanessa, whoever that is, is still here.

Who we really are is made up of so many factors. I can look at both of my parents and find things about each of them that I admire, and an equal number of things that I hate. I often wonder which of those things have manifested themselves in me. To say I have an internal battle going on inside my mind would be an understatement. There seems to be a constant struggle between what I feel called to do and what I believe others want me to do.

Both of my parents struggle with this. For one, a never-ending work cycle and ensuing accolades from colleagues mean that life is worth living. It may not always be a happy one, but as long as his efforts are in some way rewarded, he will continue to run on the gerbil wheel that his life has become. For the other, religion has become the cure-all to a life of dreams unfulfilled and goals never achieved; a salve to a damaged soul. I find myself in the middle. Although I have a strong faith, I also believe that God helps those who help themselves. Not everyone in my family shares that sentiment. For them, all things will happen in God's time, and if it doesn't happen at all, then it wasn't meant to. I would like to think that I have some control over the happenings of my life, and that although God opens doors of opportunity for me, it is I who constructed the door in the first place.

I lie on my bed, naked, in the dark. It's snowing outside, but my windows are open. I have a towel pushed under the door so my parents won't know. "We can't afford to heat the world, you know!" If I were to tell them what I was doing, they would never understand. Somewhere, I read that if you sleep naked in the cold, your body burns more calories trying to keep warm. Excellent! That's what I need to do, burn more calories. I'm at 93 pounds right now. Not good enough. My classmates are making comments about how skinny I am, but how do I know they really mean it? I have to do more so I can be more. One day I'll be perfect and then everything I've ever done wrong in my life won't matter. I am shivering and wishing I could go and take a bath to warm up. But that would make me weak, wouldn't it? I have to discipline myself. Work through the pain. Work through the fear that this is stupid . . . that it won't really work . . . that I'll get pneumonia and die. I risk it. Shaking, I run my fingertips over my rib cage. My hip bones. My thighs. Too fat. Maybe if I get up and start to exercise I'll warm up. I walk to the window to close it. Surely as long as there is some cold air coming in it will still work. But I can't risk it, so I leave the window alone. I have to do more. I feel the carpet beneath my toes. My butt. As I lie on the floor and start to do sit-ups. Up and down. Up and down. So tired. Sweating. Up and down. Up and down. Breathing hard. Time for push-ups. Elbows, white against the pink carpet. Hip bones poke into the floor as I get ready for a push-up. Up and down. Up and down. So tired. I want to quit. Lying there, panting, wanting to close my eyes and let the darkness take me away forever. So tired. So weak. So cold.

There are some things that people will not tell you. I wish they would. I don't know that anything would have changed the way I saw myself enough for me to avoid my struggles with anorexia, but I do know had someone told me about my hair falling out, my bones breaking, or my intestines failing that I might have been a little more cautious. Eating disorders are insidious. They will break you down from the inside out. Truly. There is nothing glamorous about many of the things I've had to go through in my life, yet society tells me that they are worth it if I want to look a certain way. I tell you, it's a lie.

Less than a month into group, I went into the emergency room—again. After struggling with an eating disorder for more than a decade, I made a mental decision to get well. In reality, I didn't want to have to talk about it in group. I figured if I could somehow cure myself vicariously through some of the discussions I'd had in group, then if the subject ever came up, I could honestly say it was no longer an issue.

Stupid idea number one thousand.

As a child, I often spent time talking to my mother as she was taking a bath or getting ready for the day. I remember looking at her body and feeling both admiration and disgust. I was old enough to know that her body had given me my life. Her body, with all its flaws, was beautiful. But not beautiful in the way I wanted to be beautiful. I was old enough to realize that stretch marks and excess skin were unattractive and something I feared. I would look down at my chest and imagine what it would be like to have breasts. I would run my fingers over my tight little stomach and wonder if I could ever allow myself to be pregnant—to let go of my concern over how much I weighed long enough to nurture another living soul. As early as age 9, I knew I never could. Numbers were important to me: grades, repetitions of an exercise, calories, number of chews before swallowing, and weight. To weigh 100 pounds meant, to me, certain death. There was something fatalistic about the number 100. It did not matter how old I was or how tall I was—in my mind, my weight had to be less than 100 pounds. I believed I could sustain a woman's body and all that entailed on a child's weight. How wrong I was!

"Vanessa, in our session today, I want to talk about your body and how you saw yourself as a developing young adult. When did you start to focus on the way you looked?"

Hips scared me. As a late bloomer, I did not start to get the hint of a chest (much to the delight of my peers) or hips until the end of my eighth-grade year. That was also about the time I can remember taking showers in gym class and really starting to notice different body shapes, not just who had boobs and who didn't. For the first time, I believed my body was betraying me. It seemed that each morning I would awaken to something new: chest buds, hips slowly turning outward, more definition of my facial features. I *never* gave my body permission to change, and the fact that it could change so rapidly, without my knowledge or consent, scared me to death and solidified my resolve to fight it as best I could. I weighed myself nightly and recorded my weight in my journal. If I gained any weight, I punished myself for being weak and would spend hours at night, in the dark, exercising to the point of exhaustion. If my weight did not change, I would stand in front of the mirror with a measuring tape and meticulously measure and record the width of my waist, thighs, and hips. I looked at models in magazines and silently hated them for their bodies of perfection. But it wasn't enough. I longed to be more than my body seemingly allowed me to be. And so, I did without. I denied myself food as often as I could, relishing the hunger pains that ensued. At times they were crippling. But I found that if I was strong enough and able to work through the pain, eventually they would go away. I believed my ability to do without food meant that I had more discipline than other people. But this discipline was a cause of great sorrow. How I longed for an ice cream cone sometimes or a piece of candy. And yet, to indulge in one of those treats meant a regression, a dieter's sin of epic proportions—and I could not risk it. "No, thank you" became my mantra. Hunger became my constant companion, and contrary to my initial beliefs, the tears *never, ever* stopped coming.

As a freshman in high school, I learned that if I used stimulants to go to the bathroom, I would do so more often and lose weight more quickly. True, losing waste weight is merely water weight, but in my mind, weight loss was weight loss. As a sophomore, I realized that I had the power to sabotage the food I wanted to eat by dousing it with cooking spray or heaping shortening on top of it before I could take a bite. I learned to really analyze food by its smell, texture, and taste. If I could smell a Hershey's Kiss and lick it, then I didn't have to eat it and get fat. If I prepared dinner for everyone else and then said I had already eaten, then I could get away with not eating dinner. For the first time in my life, I felt in control of my body. But my body would betray me a second time.

"When did you start your period?"

When I was sixteen. I didn't have enough body fat to start and so it took me a long time to get going. I believed that there was power in my period. That then and only then would I be seen as a woman and treated accordingly.

"How did you feel about it?"

In the books I had read, all the accounts of young girls starting their periods were romanticized. Girls became women. Boys started to notice and treated them differently. I wanted to be treated differently. I wanted a period, too. But it wasn't anything like I thought it would be! The second it came I hated it and wanted it to go away. I was told I was doomed to have a period for many years and I hated it. My periods weren't anything but painful, messy, and gross. I wanted so badly to go back in time and take my "womanhood" away, but the realization that I couldn't was completely overwhelming.

"Did people around you treat you differently?"

Yes. My brothers knew that "something" had happened and so they withdrew a little. My father stopped hugging me. It was like he knew I was different, and instead of validating me, he too withdrew his affection from me.

"So how did that affect you?"

I wanted things to go back to the way they were before my periods came. When I was a junior, I discovered diet pills. I learned that a woman's period will stop if her body fat is too low. I couldn't wait to see if that was true.

"And was it?"

Not at the beginning. My periods were all over the place to begin with, and so it was hard to tell when my cycle really was.

My senior year in high school marked the start of a new chapter of my life in more ways than one. I felt like the metamorphosis I was waiting for was taking longer than it should and so I decided I needed to take drastic action. I'd been working as a cashier at a retail store for over a year, and every chance I got I headed over to the diet aid aisle. Rows and rows of diet pills promised "immediate and long-term results." I felt like a kid in a candy store. But I knew these pills had side effects and that thought prevented me from taking them right away. But as the months passed and my unhappiness with what I saw in the mirror grew, I decided that side effects or not, I had to do something. To choose just one was an arduous task and so I resolved to try them all, one brand at a time. In the beginning, I didn't notice any difference. But as time went on, they complicated my life in a way I hadn't expected. Here again my body betrayed me.

"What do you mean?"

My caloric intake was so low that there was nothing in my body to absorb the medication in the diet pills. My behavior dramatically changed. I was so angry all the time. It seemed like no matter what anyone said to me, it was the wrong thing. I started to withdraw from everyone in my life—family, friends. I just wanted to be alone, so I could stand in front of the mirror and pinch and measure.

"Couldn't your mother see what was going on?"

You would think so, but she didn't at first. My dad had left by then, and so as a new working mother, it was all she could do to look after my younger brothers and put food on the table. She trusted me to make the right choices and to take care of myself. Part of me thought I was. Money was so tight that I believed I was doing my family a favor. If I ate less, there was more for everyone else. But there was this internal battle going on inside my head. It wasn't a matter of eating less; it was eating at all. I was using laxatives to go to the bathroom, taking diet pills, and hardly eating. My weight was right where I wanted it to be. But I still wasn't happy. I still felt like an ugly duckling and I couldn't seem to change that fact. My peers still made fun of me. Boys still ignored me. I was a complete disaster. I was thinner than I'd been before, but I still wasn't beautiful and I was hell and gone from perfect.

"Did you know you were damaging your body by using those pills and stimulants?"

I don't think I cared. I believed my weight was the most important thing in my life. If I was going to die, at least I could be thin. And a larger part of me really believed that I could stop whenever I wanted to.

"So did you?"

No. Over time, my mother started to notice the change in my behavior. She thought I was on drugs. I can remember us having a huge argument one night during my senior year in high school and her asking me point blank if I was on drugs and me denying it. I didn't consider diet pills drugs. So when I was at school one day, my mother raided my bedroom and found my boxes of diet pills. She met me at the door with the empty boxes. I have never seen her so angry in all my life. But I was angry, too. I was angry at myself for making her discovery so easy. I'd kept *all* my empty diet pill boxes as a testament to my discipline and regime. I'd tried so many different kinds and dosages over the months. If a box said to take one an hour before a meal, I took two and ate nothing. I believed I was stronger than any directives on those boxes. Over the months, I'd kept the empty boxes to know which ones I'd tried and which ones I hadn't. To know that my tracking system was now being used against me by my own mother was almost more than I could take. I can see her in my mind, shaking all of those boxes in my face, crying, asking me what I was thinking. I told her I hated her and that she was interfering in something she knew nothing about. She literally dragged me into the doctor's office and I was held down for a blood test to see which drugs were in my system. She cried. I cried. But the doctor said nothing. I thought for sure I was busted, but he didn't say anything. I promised to stop and that was the end of it.

"Did you want it to be?"

Part of me did. I was on a gerbil wheel of my own creation, and I couldn't get off. Even though I said I hated my mother for what she'd done, deep down inside I was grateful to her for caring enough about me to bring what I'd been doing to light. Maybe a part of me was trying to get caught so I wouldn't have to keep up the pace and lies anymore. But when the doctor said nothing, I knew my hopes of getting off the wheel were misguided. In fact, it was like the second my mother and I left that office, someone hit a hyperspeed switch.

"So did you stop?"

Hell no! If my own doctor wasn't going to make me stop, then I wasn't going to show weakness by stopping on my own. No. This whole episode just forced me to be even more secretive about my behavior. I hated myself for being careless enough to get caught and punished myself by eating even less and working out even more. It wasn't until I was in college that I stopped using the pills. They just weren't working for me the way I thought they should and so I started doing enemas, too. I never imagined those would open the door for complications ten years after the fact.

"So do you know how you went from using diet pills and stimulants to having to go to the ER because your body was poisoning itself? Do you see any connection here? On some level you had to know what you were doing to your body was unhealthy."

Maybe there is a part of me that feels untouchable. I've abused my body for so long without consequences that I suppose over time I thought there wouldn't ever be any. Did I know what I was doing was unhealthy? Yes. Did I care? No. Not if it meant I lost more weight. In my defense, though, I didn't know that by using stimulants for so long, if I were ever to just stop, my body would go into shock.

"So, is that what happened to you, Vanessa?"

Yes.

"Why have you not talked to me about this in our sessions? I'm here to help you—remember that. I may not have been able to do anything to stop what was going to happen, but I hope you realize that you missed an opportunity for help. You are *not* alone. You don't have to be stoic and fight this all by yourself. Talk to me. Tell me what happened. How did you end up in the ER?"

You don't know how humiliating this is.

"No, I don't. So I want you to tell me. What happened?"

Several weeks ago, I stopped using any stimulants to go to the bathroom. I really believed I didn't need them anymore.

By the doctor's best estimates, I managed to go for nearly two weeks without going to the bathroom. My hair and skin started to exude toxic by-products that saturated my body. I could not sleep. I could not eat. And finally, I could not drink. Anything.

I had been "too busy" to go to the bathroom at any time over the previous two weeks. In all honesty, though, the urge never hit me. I didn't realize that without stimulation it never would. My body was so accustomed to chemicals making it work that once those were taken away, it no longer remembered how to work on its own.

By the time I got to the ER, my body had started to shut down. All attempts by it to warn me over the previous two weeks had all but gone unnoticed. My body, literally, was taking things into its own hands.

The doctor told me: "I don't know if we can get you through this, Vanessa. We will try to do what we can, but things are looking pretty grim. We are going to run some tests and see if we can't get you cleaned out. This is going to take a while, so you're going to have to be patient."

I had no energy to do anything but nod.

My mother had flown in to help take care of me. I didn't want her to see how far I'd fallen, but there was nothing I could do to hide it.

As always, I'd put everything in my life ahead of my own needs: husband, work, pets. I had such a hard time with giving myself permission to do anything for myself, even take a shit, without feeling bad about it. I never knew being so selfless could be so damaging.

Together, my mother and I waited six hours in the waiting room. A sea of stab victims, car accident casualties, and babies came in waves through the ER doors. The ER was full. One ambulance after another screeched to a halt, threw open its doors, unloaded its cargo, and then took off again for another pickup. I tried to look as nonchalantly as I could at the other people waiting, trying to figure out why they were here, what was wrong with them. More than once, I caught other people looking at me, trying to do the same thing.

"Vanessa. I need you to change into this gown and wait here. Someone from radiology will be right here for you. We're looking for a blockage, Vanessa, or a twist in your intestines. If we find one, you'll need surgery. Cross your fingers we don't."

Blackness.

Lead vest.

"Hold your breath. Don't move."

Snap.

"Okay. We're turning you over."

Lead vest.

"Hold your breath. Don't move."

Snap.

"Okay. One more. Other side."

Lead vest.

"Hold your breath. Don't move."

Snap.

Lights. Moving down the hall on a gurney. Looking up at the lights on the ceiling as they fly by. My eyes close. The voices start again.

Well, isn't this just a fine state of affairs? Come on, Vanessa. How many more times are we going to go through this? Here it is Christmas Eve. Look at where you are. What are you doing? How are you going to explain this? Do you know how embarrassing this is? It's one thing to be out of control. It's another to have the whole world know it. I can't believe you. Who knows how much this is going to cost. And you know the pathetic part? You did this to yourself. Great. Another brilliant idea of yours goes awry.

I don't know when the tears started, but by the time I got back to my room, I couldn't see clearly.

My mother arrived. "Well, what did they say?"

They just did some X-rays, Mom. Someone should be in shortly to talk to us.

Waiting.

Looking at my nails.

My socks.

The floor.

Anything to not have to talk about me and why we're here.

A nurse came in and threw some clear bags and liquid on the counter.

Someone came in with a portable toilet. "Okay. We're going to try this first. I need you to get on your hands and knees with your butt in the air. We're going to start trying to flush you out, okay? The X-rays showed you have waste backing up into your rib cage."

Tears dotted the tissue paper of the bed as I tried to get into position. Humiliation doesn't even begin to cover it.

A code blue was called over the loudspeaker and the nurse rushed out.

"Be right back!"

But she never did come back.

After half an hour, Mom and I decided that if this was going to get done, it would be because we did it ourselves. My mom began to do something for me, her oldest child, that no one else in the world would: an enema. I counted ten of them before I stopped counting.

Soap and water. Full. Wait. Release. Again.

For four hours.

And you know the sad thing?

Nothing happened! Absolutely nothing. Just water. That's it. This wasn't working, and I was becoming so dehydrated from not being able to drink anything that my vision blurred.

I have never been so mad at myself and so embarrassed at the same time.

By the time the nurse came back, I had been in the ER for nearly twelve hours.

"Things are not going as we had planned, Vanessa. You will need to go home and drink this. Be careful; it should start working in about an hour."

Not true.

I drank the magic cure, took a shower, and slept for eight hours before it started working. That's how full of waste I really was.

Twenty-four hours later, I was still going to the bathroom. But for the first time in weeks, I was feeling better. The scale would show I had lost 20 pounds in one day.

———————

"That's amazing. The question is, how do we make sure you *never* get yourself in this position again?"

I don't know that I fully understand how I got there *this* time.

"So, how did that experience make you feel?"

Horrible. I've always thought that what I did to myself was okay and no one else's business because it didn't affect anyone. But this was different. My husband, my mother, my stepfather, and my in-laws were all affected by my actions because their holiday celebrations were preempted. So, not only did I feel embarrassed about the whole ordeal but I felt bad because I had become a source of frustration to lots of other people. The bottom line was I had done that to myself. Not on purpose per se, but it could have been avoided. My ER visit was the culmination of years of bodily abuse and neglect. I couldn't hide this. I couldn't fix it on my own. I couldn't justify it by saying that it was okay because no one else was involved. *Lots* of people were involved, and it made me feel selfish and small. But I also felt betrayed. My body was supposed to keep what I did to it a secret and it didn't. I thought it was possible to trick my body into subservience. I thought I was in charge of it. But I learned very quickly that if I don't care for my body, I will lose control over it. I feel trapped.

"How are you trapped? You have a functioning body."

I think sometimes my discipline has allowed me to feel overly confident about my abilities to get my body to do what I want it to do. I've trained it not to be hungry or to need as much sleep. I feel totally blindsided by the whole "eliminate waste" thing. It never crossed my mind that by ignoring what it was trying to tell me, I could die. I might be more disciplined than other people about what I put into my body, but if I don't get rid of what's in it, all the discipline in the world won't matter. How humbling is that?

Once the holidays were over, I did have to talk about what happened to me in group. The whole idea of curing myself was an avoidance behavior and something that prompted a new topic of discussion.

"Tonight we're going to talk about caretaking. Each of you is very nurturing toward others, but neglectful of many of your own personal needs. Does anyone know where this might come from?"

A pause.

A deafening silence brought on by four women living in denial.

"Nyla, food is an issue for you. Do you feel stronger not accepting any?"

Nyla looks up.

"I don't know."

"Yes, you do. Think about the work that you've been doing. Your ideas of food are changing, are they not?"

"Yes."

"Well, let's look at food as a method of caretaking. You need food to survive, yet you only allow yourself a little food at certain times. How do you know when you deserve food?"

"When I feel good about myself, then I think it's okay to eat. If I've made a mistake or let someone down, then I feel like I need to be punished or something and that takes my appetite away."

"Okay. That's a good start. Why don't you write about that? Now, Sarah. Sex has to do with caretaking for you. Do you want to talk about that?"

"I want to be close to someone. I want to feel like I'm loved. My mom wasn't ever around and I didn't know my dad, so I had to get affection from other people. When I was little, I was sexually molested by one of my neighbors. I didn't know what was going on, but I remember him telling me that he loved me and that he thought I was beautiful. He said I was an angel. That's what I had always wanted to hear, but there wasn't ever anyone around to tell me. So I tried to find people who thought that way about me. When I was in high school, I found out that if I let a guy finger me, then I was loved and beautiful. But the more it happened, the more I didn't feel loved or beautiful. I felt dirty. So I started to hide in my mind. I wanted to feel all of the closeness but I didn't like the way it made me feel."

"So, how do you take care of yourself? How do you make yourself feel better?"

"It depends. Sometimes I drink. Sometimes I smoke a joint. Sometimes I just curl up on the couch with my cat and a movie. It depends on how bad I feel and how desperate I am to feel better."

"That's a good start. I want you to write down some other ways in which you try to make yourself feel better and then we'll come back to you."

"All right, Vanessa. Let's talk about taking care of yourself."

What do you want to know?

"I want to know how you were taken care of when you were little. Did you feel safe? I want you to write about your relationship with your parents. What types of caretaking behavior did you learn from them? How did you see them taking care of themselves?"

I stare at the sheet of notebook paper in front of me. It mocks me, waiting to be filled with memories buried for many years. Like a high diver, I plunge into the past.

My mom did an excellent job of making sure that I was clean, had food, and was given warm clothes to wear. My mom was an excellent caretaker. She was the best nurse I could ever hope for. She always made sure that I was comfortable and that I had the right medicines. My father thought illness was for the weak. I don't ever remember him taking medicine—for anything. He was never sick, and if he was, he felt like he could tough it out. It made me feel bad when I was sick and wasn't strong enough to tough it out.

As a child I was always hurt in one way or another—scraped knees, stubbed toes, bruises from running into things, something. Part of me hated being hurt, but the other part of me was a big wuss. I had no pain tolerance, and the second I hurt myself, I ran off crying for a bandage. Bandages made things better. If I couldn't see the cut, then it didn't hurt as much. Plus, if it was covered up, I couldn't keep jacking with it. I was fascinated with scabs and how they formed. If I had a cut and it wasn't covered, I would mess with it—pick off the scab and watch it bleed. I have numerous scars on my legs from things that I just wouldn't let heal as a child. Bandages also showed the world I was hurt. I didn't have to say anything. A person could see the bandage and know that there was pain there. Bandages promised unsolicited sympathy.

In elementary school, Tuesdays were track days. That was the day we would leave the gymnasium behind and run laps around a black, asphalt track. This was a problem, because more often than not, I wore dresses and Mary Jane shoes to school. Sometimes I remembered track day, and other times I didn't. On the days that I didn't, I would have to run anyway. My peers would sail past me on the track wearing their tennis shoes, and I would become frustrated at the lack of speed my Mary Jane shoe's contained. So I would run—faster and faster until I could catch up with them. And then it would happen. I would hit the loose gravel pile in the corner of one edge of the track. Because the rocks were all black, it was hard to know which pieces were melted down and which were loose. But my shoes had no problem finding out which rocks were which. My Mary Jane shoes would hit those rocks and down I'd go—hands out in front of me like I was sliding into home base, my chin hitting the track and my palms, elbows, and kneecaps absorbing most of the slide. The crash was immediate and stole my breath. By the time I realized I was on the ground, I could see my classmates finishing up their laps and staring at me. More often than not, the gym teacher would come tearing back in my direction to scoop me up and dust me off. But dusting wasn't enough. I hit the track with such force that the small, black rocks were imbedded in my palms and knees. By the time I was back on my feet, a steady throbbing was pulsating through my legs. It was off to the nurse's office, again, for her tweezers and Mercurochrome. I tried to be brave, but I couldn't. The tears came out in sobs and I secretly hated myself for being such a klutz. I hated my gym teacher for making me run. And I hated my stupid Mary Jane shoes for causing me to slip. Hobbling home, stiff legged, with the big, white gauze bandages on my knees brought me unwanted attention from the other kids at school. I wanted to be seen as a mature person, not some baby who couldn't fight gravity. Those were the first times I can remember other kids laughing at me, at something I'd done, at something I felt like I couldn't control.

Once I got home, my knees were the source of great concern, and, as a result, extra attention. I can remember walking stiff legged so I wouldn't have to bend my knees. It seemed like bending them caused even more pain, so I walked like a soldier as long as I could before my parents told me I was being ridiculous and to walk like a normal person.

How I hated having those bandages removed for bath time! My wounds had wept during the day and glued themselves to the surface of the cotton pads. Ripping off the bandages meant ripping off my scabs and it was horribly painful. (Although the end results are the same, picking a scab and controlling the pain is not the same as having it pulled off because it's stuck to a bandage.) My mother was a pick-a-corner-and-rip! type of person, whereas I was an inch-by-inch, easy-off person. Rarely could we come to an agreement about the method of bandage removal, and so more than once, I was brought to tears not only for the injuries I had suffered but also for the added injury of having my bandages removed. I wanted to do it my way, and that didn't seem to be the right way. So I learned to do things a little earlier than other people expected me to.

I figured out that if I did something early and was then asked about it, I could say it had already been done and wouldn't be corrected for it. But if I waited, then I was at the mercy of the person doing the asking. If I were to safeguard my way, then I would have to be on alert—paying attention to every-thing going on around me so I could time when I did certain things. That way, I could take care of myself and my needs in my own way. If I cried, then no one else had to know I was weak. If I was too rough and made the hurt worse, then I could doctor myself and no one else would know. And if I was mad and thinking bad things about someone else, I could whisper them out loud and wouldn't get into trouble for them. I truly believed that what other people didn't know wouldn't hurt them. I never imagined that it might come back to haunt me.

It seems like such an innocent establishment of behavior, but this whole concept would give me the skills I would need to keep self-destructive behaviors a secret in the years to come. By showering early, eating early, and going to bed early, I was able to preserve my way without anyone else knowing about it. I *didn't know it at the time, but all this secrecy goes back to the second grade for me and all those skinned knees and elbows. Interesting.*

––––––––––––

I am four years old. I want to be a ballerina, so I've been placed in a class at the Houston School of Classical Ballet. The halls are filled with girls running around with their hair in buns wearing pink tights and black leotards. Some are stretching on the floor or asking a friend to help them to get their feet up over their heads. For the first time, I realize I can see bones on other people. I've seen my mother naked many times and never seen her bones the way I can see them on these girls. I think their bones are beautiful. I look down at my little body. A Pooh-bear tummy and skinny little chicken legs. I feel surrounded by princesses and I want to be just like them.

"Girls!"

An older woman in a leotard and a tissue-paper skirt slams a walking stick on the ground. "Let's begin. Line up at the barre. And here we go!"

She nods to a man behind a piano. "Maestro, please! Watch me carefully. And first position. No! Don't look at your feet! Again. First position. Good. And again."

I close my eyes for a moment and listen to the man playing the piano. He is playing a song I have heard my father play before. I open my eyes to catch a glimpse of myself in a bank of floor-to-ceiling mirrors that line the wall. In my mind, I am just like the prima ballerinas I have seen on public television, and for the first time in my life, I feel graceful. I imagine being on a stage in front of a crowd of thousands cheering just for me, and I put my feet together and go through the second position.

"And again. Suck in your stomachs! No one wants to see a fat ballerina! And again. Now girls! We're going to work on our hands and feet together. Watch closely. Nadia! Would you come to the front and show our new girls how it's done? Beautiful. And again. Very nice. All right, are we ready to try it?"

My heart feels warm inside. The music is slow and graceful. The older girls move their bodies like reeds in the wind. I look at them and try to imitate what I see.

"Vanessa! What are you doing? Look at your form! You are not *a dancer! There is supposed to be grace in your movements! Your butt is too big! You look*

like the Hamburglar from McDonald's. You could put a tray on your butt and carry hamburgers!" She begins to waddle like a duck.

"Look at me! Girls! You must suck your stomach and butt in or else you will look like Vanessa over here! Now let's practice! And one. And two. And again."

But I don't hear any more. The warmth I'd felt in my heart just moments before is now gone and replaced with something that feels like a rock. When I look at the mirror again, I no longer look beautiful. For the first time, I'd been called fat and I've never forgotten it.

My mother was diagnosed as being diabetic when I was six years old, and for the first time in my life, food was a topic of discussion. Up until that point, food was just that—food. It wasn't interesting, it wasn't exciting, it was just food. I remember mealtimes as being family time. I was just barely old enough to start helping my mother in the kitchen by setting the table or helping her unload the dishwasher. I felt proud of these skills and tried to do them as best I could.

But when my mother was diagnosed, mealtimes became something else— purposeful.

There were new tools in the kitchen now. A scale. A food pyramid. Special- ized cookbooks. New foods I hadn't seen before. And a new group of "bad" or "forbidden" foods.

I was old enough to read on my own and could see how the labels of these new foods were different from those of some of the other foods we'd had before. Not one for junk food, my mother had always carefully controlled which snacks my brothers and I had access to, and how much of them we ate. But now there were new snack foods. Fruit snacks. Granola bars. Cheese and crackers. For the first time ever, I saw diet cola in the refrigerator. Our Kool-Aid was now sugar free, and store-bought snacks were replaced with things my mother made from scratch: Chex mix, Rice Krispies Treats, popcorn. If I brought candy home from a birthday party, it was promptly thrown away. Gum? Forget it. Never!

I saw, for the first time, my mother paying attention to things called calo- ries, and I didn't understand why. I couldn't see how some foods were good and others were bad. I didn't understand why I could eat as much as I wanted, but my mother had to measure her portions. I didn't understand why if my *mother went to a school party with me she never had anything to eat. If you offered her punch, she would say, "No, thank you." If you offered her cake, she would say, "No, thank you." And so I started to believe that she was stronger than the rest of the world. Whereas everyone else was saying yes and eating all of these snacks, my mother was strong enough to say no. I wanted to be strong, too.*

It was a gradual thing at first: not eating donuts after church services, not eating cake or ice cream at birthday parties, or eating anything that I thought would make me weak. Through my saying no, I believed I was exhibiting a greater level of self-discipline than most people were capable of. It was shocking and exhilarating at the same time.

This denial of want would not fully manifest itself until I was in high school. By then, I'd made the connection between physical appearance and eating habits, and by then, I wanted to be perfect—perfectly thin, that is.

———————

I am six. My brothers are in the bedroom and it's time for dinner. I walk into the kitchen to see what we're having and no one is there. That's when I hear my father's voice in the living room, as he kneels next to my mother, who is lying on the couch.

"Donna! Donna! Wake up! Come on. Let's wake up now. Donna!"

She had laid down for a nap a while ago, but it was dinnertime and she hadn't even started cooking yet.

"Donna!"

I want to turn and run, but at that very moment, my father catches me out of the corner of his eye.

"Vanessa! I need you to get a glass of orange juice from the kitchen. Don't cry, just do it! Donna! I need you to open your eyes for me. Do you hear me? Donna?"

Crying, I hand my father the glass.

"Here's some juice for you. Come on. Just a little bit. Vanessa, see if you can help me sit her up."

I want to help, but my mother is so heavy in my little arms.

"Donna! I need you to sit up for me and drink some of this. Come on. Vanessa, quit crying! It's going to be okay. Your mother is just having a reaction."

A muffled, incoherent voice comes from the couch.

"Donna . . . come on . . . that's it. A little more juice, come on. You can do it. That's it. Good." My father continues to hold my mother.

"Vanessa, I need you to take care of your brothers for a few minutes. I need to get your mom up and walking. I'll get dinner going in a few minutes. Why don't you set the table, okay?"

I nod and run out of the room. I can't stop crying. I thought my mother was going to die.

I'm shaking. My brothers are playing on the floor with wooden blocks. They have no idea what is going on. In any other circumstance, I would take delight in knowing I knew a secret and had been my father's helper. But not today. My mother's illness is not a secret I want, but it's one I must keep so I don't upset my brothers unnecessarily.

I lie on my bed and try to erase the images that I've just seen.

She just laid there. Not moving. Not talking. Not doing anything. She was sleeping, but she looked dead. Lifeless.

I crawl up on my bed in a fetal position. I feel cold. Even my stuffed animals don't comfort me. I face the wall so my brothers won't see me crying. I can hear them behind me and long for the naiveté they possess.

I wish someone would come in and hold me. Make me feel better and reassure me that this won't happen again.

But no one comes.

I can't stop crying, but I have to be quiet. If my dad hears me, he'll be mad. He has too much to deal with already.

What if she dies? What if I'm totally alone forever?

I want to crawl in a hole and wait there for someone to find me. To scoop me out and hold me tight. But I know that won't ever happen. I'm the oldest. I'm the one who is supposed to be the big helper of the family.

Doesn't my mom know how scared I am? My dad doesn't like tears. He doesn't know what to do to make me feel better when I cry.

But my mom should know. Her mommy sense should tell her that I'm afraid and crying and shaking.

She should come to me and hold me.

But she doesn't.

A small part of me died that day. For the first time in my life, I realized what my mother was dealing with. This wasn't just a diet. Or special foods. Or saying no. This was her life. One that could be taken away at any time, and it shocked me. I thought parents were supposed to live forever. I learned that day that isn't true. I also learned that at one of the scariest moments of my life, the only person in the world who was free to comfort me was me. And it's been that way ever since.

"So, **Vanessa,** you've talked about having to comfort yourself through a very scary time. It's hard when a child learns that her parent is suffering from an illness that may be fatal. Did that change your relationship with your mother at all?"

Definitely. But I couldn't let her know it. I thought if she knew that I was pulling back from her a little, she would take it personally and hold it against me. Even though I knew her disease wasn't her fault, I didn't understand it and never again felt 100 percent confident that I could count on her to always be there for me. I grew up a lot that day.

"Was she sick all the time?"

Not all the time, but when she was sick, it was life-threatening. More than once, I have had to call 911 for her because I couldn't get her to wake up. She has been near death several times, and there have been multiple occasions when the doctors have told us there was no hope. Most people mourn their parents just once. I feel like I've mourned mine several times over. Every incident brought out a new level of fear in me—fear that I would be alone, fear that I hadn't shown my mother what a wonderful person I'd turned out to be, fear that there were things she needed to teach me and didn't have the chance, fear that one day I'd be like her and leave my loved ones behind too.

"So connect this back to comforting yourself."

Well, I learned that I had to handle things myself. I had to be the one who solved my own problems, because she may not be there to help me through them. If I was hurting, I didn't want to say anything because I didn't want her to worry about me, die, and then wonder for all eternity how things turned out.

"So when you hurt yourself, what did you do to make yourself feel better?"

Do we really have to talk about that again?

"Yes, that's why you're here. We talked about what you do; now we need to find out *why* you do some of the things you do."

After everything is done, it's like my vision clears. When I'm cutting, I don't really see it. I mean, I know that something is happening, but I don't really absorb *what* is happening. But once I am able to really see what I've done, then I usually cry—again. Because I'm sorry. Because I hate that I've done it. Because I am shocked at what it looks like and panicked as to how I'm going to explain it.

But just like there is a ritual before I begin, there is a ritual after it's over.

"And what does that involve?"

The first part has to do with cleanup. Not of me, but of the tools. I have to make sure that there aren't any signs of what I've been doing. So, I take alcohol swabs and clean up the scissors or razor blades or whatever and put them away. I rinse out the sink. I make sure that I empty the bathroom trash so that there's no evidence there either. Then, and only then, can I focus on me.

Just like there are voices that tell me to cut, there are voices that tell me it's okay. They are softer, kinder voices. They reassure me that I'm not a bad person. That I'm not a freak. That I am loved and going to be okay.

I focus on my breathing.

In and out.

Deep and consistent.

I look at myself in the eyes and try to see what's really there—in deep behind my irises. I want to see if there is any change. Perhaps I've transformed into this horrible person and don't know it yet. So I look. I force myself to really look into my own eyes—something I rarely do.

And I wait.

The pain eventually comes. Maybe it's two minutes, maybe it's ten. It's almost like until the pain starts, I forget that I've even been hurt. But once the pain starts, then I start making myself feel better. I clean my wounds, gingerly, carefully, lovingly. If there is a loose piece of skin, I tear it away. It sounds weird, but I want the cuts to look nice. I don't want them to appear jagged and random. Nothing about what I do is random!

Once I've cleaned everything up, I usually take a shower. A ritualistic cleaning of my person.

And that's it.

"Are you sure?"

Yeah.

"What happens after you get out of the shower?"

Oh. That.

Well, I dress my wounds. I find the bandages that will cover them the most and open them. I take out the antibiotic cream and apply it, with a swab, to my cuts. Then I put the bandages on and I wrap myself in my own arms. I hold myself in a way that no one came in and held me all those many years ago. It's weird. I'm thirty-five years old, yet I feel about six at that moment. If I could, I would get a stuffed animal and blanket and go lie down. I mean, how weird is that?

"It's not weird at all."

How can you say that?

"Think about it, Vanessa. You are comforting yourself. You are reverting to a time when you needed comfort and none was given. You are reassuring yourself that even in a time of deep pain, you will be okay. It's a very powerful process."

That's great, but how old am I going to have to be before I know that I'm okay? I'm old enough now that I have a support network outside my parents. If they aren't there for me, then it should be okay because I have enough other people who are.

"Rationally speaking, that makes sense. But we're not talking about a rational behavior. We're talking about something that is deeply emotional and rooted in something that happened to you years ago. That childlike part of yourself needs to be held. It needs to be reassured that it isn't alone and that it is cared for. You are doing that for yourself because at a critical time, it wasn't done for you."

But I feel bad about that. My mom did an excellent job comforting me during other times.

"Yes, but perhaps by then it was already too late. You said by the age of 6 or so, you'd already been faced with this reality. Part of you shut off. Not all of you, just part of you. This is the part we are trying to work on."

A silence envelops the room.

"What about your father?"

What about him?

"Was he there for you? Did he comfort you like your mother did?"

Only when I was really small.

"Tell me about that."

We had this huge rocking chair in the living room of our house. It was wide enough for my dad and me to sit side by side on it sometimes. It was tan, a woven fabric with orange and dark brown strings. It had dark wood arms, oak probably. My mother had made white crocheted doilies for the headrest. I remember it because it flopped when we rocked.

When I was small, I would crawl into my dad's lap and we would tummy rock. I would bear-hug him and he would tuck my little feet under his legs. My head fit into the crook of his neck perfectly, and we would rock. It was my favorite position.

One time, it was raining outside and the power went out. I had to have been age 2 1/2 or 3 because I can't be sure that my younger brother was born yet. I remember everyone but my dad had gone to bed. I had a bad dream and I remember walking into the living room, my feet slapping the wood part of the floor as I went in. It was a total downpour. One of those that shake the windowpanes and make the tree branches dance on the sides of the house. I was afraid and really wanted my dad to hold me . . . to rock me back to sleep. The house was pitch dark. I thought I heard my dad in the living room, and so that was where I went. But as soon as I went in, a tremendous flash of lightning illuminated the room and revealed it was completely empty. I was terrified. I ran back to my room and cried.

Part of me wanted to go into my parents' room and wake him up so he could rock me. But a larger part of me told me I had better not. So, I didn't.

I think that was the last time I ever wanted my dad to rock me. I'm sure he did after that, but I never wanted it more than I did that rainy night and he wasn't there.

"Did he comfort you at other times?"

It just depended. My dad was from the "tough it out" school of life. He wasn't interested in a lot of sob stories or excuses. If you were sick, get better. If you had a problem, fix it. If you had a conflict with someone, deal with it. He wasn't nurturing the way my mother was. His type of nurturing was more subtle. He was one who would bring me flowers for my birthday or take me to see his office at the university. You felt valuable being in his presence because he was so busy and so important, you knew he could spend his time with anyone. So, if he spent it with you, then it meant you were somebody special.

"Did you feel special?"

Not usually.

I'm telling you, I was the disappointment. I always felt like a lot was expected of me and despite my best efforts, I fell short. My parents expected perfection. Something I could never give them, no matter how hard I tried. And you know the funny part? I kept trying. Most people would say to hell with it and give up. But not me. Oh no, I had to keep pushing myself harder and harder to try to reach a goal that was unattainable, at best. It's like inside I knew it was unrealistic, but I was so convinced that if I worked hard enough I could make it happen. But over time, I realized I would never live up to my parents' expectations and I believed I could see their disappointment in me, their eldest child, in their eyes and hear it in the tone of their voice. The inner feelings of defeat were so strong and they had nowhere to go. I hurt so badly on the inside for the person I wanted to be and others expected me to be. But in the end, I was only me and it never seemed to be good enough. There weren't enough apologies in the world to make up for that fact. And so I sought out a way to punish myself because that's what I thought I deserved.

———————

I am nine years old. The closet is dark. Only a thin ribbon of light streams in from under the door. I know if I am caught in here, there will be hell to pay. My ears strain for sounds of footsteps. My heart races. What if the door is opened? What will I say? How can I possibly explain what I am doing in my parents' closet? I have to hurry. I can't let anyone know I'm in here or what I'm doing. I sit on the floor and feel the carpet under my legs. It itches. The air reeks of leather, shoe polish, and my mother's L'Air du Temps. My fingers know exactly where to find the object I came for.

The shoe feels heavy in my hand. It isn't mine. I turn it over and feel the hard leather beneath my fingers. I feel my right arm and close my eyes. I imagine hearing it snap. My teeth are clenched. My blood is boiling. I hold my breath and try not to scream as I repeatedly hit my wrist and arm. I feel like I could kill someone. My head hurts from crying and from banging it against the floor. I put the shoe down and feel my arm for blood. None. That pisses me off. Why doesn't the damn thing break? Time is running out and I'm still furious. I must do more. I pick up the shoe and begin to hit my thighs until they are numb. I wait for my blood pressure to go down and it doesn't. I have to keep going. If I were a good girl, I wouldn't be so angry. Anger isn't allowed and I have to make it go away. I grab the shoe again and start to hit. My wrist. My forearm. My elbow. Again and again. I strain to hear a snap, but there is none. Why can't my best ever be good enough? I want to hit something so hard it is destroyed. I keep hitting my arm. My thighs are pulsating and throbbing feverishly. My arm is tender to the touch. I put the shoe back where I got it from. His shoe. I feel my breathing slow. My tears have crusted on my cheeks. I close my eyes. There. Maybe this is good enough. I want to yell, "See, I can do something right!" I cannot tell my father how much I hate him or how angry I am at him for making me feel inadequate, but I can defile something of his and take pleasure in knowing I did stand up for myself even if it was in the dark. I am exhausted. I slowly open the door and see that swollen, raised welts have appeared on my thighs and arm. The blood vessels near my wrist have broken. Stealthily, I move toward my bedroom. There, behind closed doors, I will reassure myself that I am not spine-

less. That I am good enough. That I can do something right, even if it is hurt. That seems to be what I do best. Only now, I can hurt as much on the outside as I do on the inside. I believe I have appropriate feelings, even if there is never a chance to express them and be heard. I feel like I was heard today. My body heard me as I was shouting my hate in silence.

My father is a genius. He's someone who can make something out of nothing. He's your all-American success story. Local farm boy does well. Gets good grades. Goes to college on a full scholarship. Defies the odds and digs himself out of the shithole that is his birthright. My mother, another success story. Her parents were completely inept, yet she was smart enough to educate herself. She taught herself how to cook. How to make clothes by hand. How to quilt. How to be a good parent, even when she had no role model to follow. My teachers. Here were people who could be anything in the world and they chose to plant seeds in little cups and were just as amazed as I was. And then there was me. No matter what I did, someone around me could always do it better. If I played a song on the piano, here would come my father, who "hadn't touched a keyboard in twenty years," to play it ten times better than I could—from memory! If I tried to draw something, he could do it better. My little brother, a phenomenal artist, started taking classes at the Houston Museum of Art when he was five. If I tried to sew something in my home economics class, here came my mother to "help me fix it." I was too stupid to even know it needed to be fixed! The only thing I knew I could do was write. So I did. And dammit if my father didn't try to come behind me and make it better . . . make it his . . . make it totally unrecognizable as my own work.

When I wrote the story "How I Climbed Mt. Rainier," I was nine years old and in the fifth grade. My family had just moved from Texas. It was my first year in Washington and I was having a hard time adjusting to being the new kid in school. It seemed like the only time the kids wanted to talk to me was to hear my accent.

"Go on, Vanessa. Say 'state.'"

State.

"Oh, that's great. Stay-ate."

"You're a hoot!"

And then they would leave me wherever I was, alone.

I was never invited to play at recess. In fact, I made it a point to bring a book to school every day so I could find a quiet place outside and read, praying for classes to start again soon.

But when I wasn't reading, I was writing.

I started to keep a journal that year, and into it I poured my deepest thoughts and desires. I didn't know how to make people like me, and I was still trying to figure out how to make my parents proud of me.

I don't know how I heard about the writing contest, but when I did, I knew just the story I wanted to share.

The heroine in my story was everything I wasn't, which was strong, confident, and accomplished. In the story, I pretend that I am a mountain climber, the youngest to ever climb Mt. Rainier. Nothing dramatic, but hardly your unicorn and fluffy bunny story that most nine-year-old writings are composed of.

I won first place.

I was asked to rewrite my story in my best cursive so that it might be housed in one of the university collections. I spent an entire week of lunches making my story into a handwritten masterpiece.

As the winner, I was asked to attend a young writer's workshop at one of the area universities. Once there, I met some of the most famous young adult writers and illustrators of the time. I knew instantly that was what I wanted to do. I didn't know how yet, but I knew there would come a day when I too would be showing young people how to be a successful writer.

I won first place in that writing contest for the next three years. I prided myself in upping the ante with my stories each year and really believed that I was honing my craft.

The summer of my sixth-grade year, a summer camp was offered for young writers. It was very expensive, and unlike the church camp I usually attended, there were no scholarships available.

I begged and pleaded to go to this camp. I offered to give up my birthday and babysitting money to help pay for it. Finally, my parents relented and I was allowed to go.

It was one of the most powerful weeks of my life.

Finally, I felt like I belonged. I was surrounded by other kids who enjoyed words as much as I did, and it opened my eyes to a new world of possibilities.

I continued to write in my journal each night. When I could, I wrote poem after poem and numerous short stories. Some I shared with others; most I did not.

But I saved them all, praying that one day I would become a strong enough writer that I could go back and refine my work. For the first time in my life, I had real confidence in my abilities. My teachers told me I had a gift, and I believed them.

But all of that changed my eighth-grade year.

That year, I asked my father to go to the writing conference with me. My story had won first place yet again, and because of age restrictions, this would be my last opportunity to attend. I wanted my father to be there, with me, to share in something I had created.

But to him, it wasn't good enough.

"Let's rework this, Vanessa."

The story was already accepted. That's the one I have to turn in.

"No one is going to know. I really think we can work together and make this stronger, okay? You want this to be the best, right?"

Silently, I died a little inside.

I already thought I was the best. I mean, isn't that what first place meant? Not this time.

When my father said he and I would work together, that meant he would rewrite it and I would sit there and watch. I didn't understand why my story needed to be fixed, and I didn't understand why my dad felt like he was at liberty to fix it. I saw my story undergo a massive transformation. By the time he was done with it, it was completely unrecognizable.

My father was so proud of how far my story had come.

"Well, what do you think? Now, isn't this much better?"

I took it and walked away mumbling thanks.

When I got back to my room, I cried. Once again, my best wasn't enough. Once again, I had fallen short. Once again, I felt like a failure and I no longer wanted to go to the writing conference. What was there to share with my dad? I wanted to share my story, my accomplishment, with him. Now, we would be celebrating his *story.*

Dammit, why couldn't I stand up for myself? I know why! My protests would be met with a head-shaking, I-can't-believe-you're-making-such-a-big-deal-out-of-this look. Eye rolling. Exasperated sigh. Why couldn't I tell my dad what I thought? What I wanted? Because I'd be told how ungrateful I was! Does he not know how hard I'd worked to make my story wonderful and how angry I am that he didn't see that? No! And what's really sad is, he doesn't care! All I want is for him to be proud of me and still I am left wanting. Even though he *is the one who crossed a boundary and offered help where none was wanted, I am the one made to feel guilty. Shouldn't I want my father's help? Is it even remotely possible that his ideas were better than mine? No! His offering help meant that my ideas weren't good enough. Maybe he believes my story won by default, that the other stories were so poor mine had to win. Even in victory, I feel like a complete disappointment. It's official.* Nothing *I do will ever be good enough. My hands have balled themselves into fists. At some point, they started hitting the tops of my thighs, numbing my mind to the reality of my failure as a writer, but bringing it back around to the very real pain stemming from my extremities. Opening my hands, I notice my nails. Like claws, they tear at my flesh, leaving long marks across my thighs. These instantly turn a deep shade of purple. I've managed to pull small pieces of skin away and blood pools in small droplets. I smile. I know that by tomorrow these places will have scabbed over and I will pick at them until the scar tissue prevents me from doing so any longer.*

"Tonight we're going to discuss punishment. Each of you is involved in some form of self-punishment, and hopefully I can help you understand why and where that comes from. The hard part about tonight's assignment is that I don't want you to focus on the punishment itself. I want you to think about the situation and the feelings *you* believe were behind the punishment. What was the message in the punishment? You can tell about what happened to you and the consequence, but I want to see if you can put yourself in your parents' shoes and make any connections to your own behavior, okay?"

I don't want to keep writing about these painful parts of my past. Yes, I'm making connections, but I really don't know if the connections are worth the hurt of the feelings these remembrances bring up.

As always, I'm sitting in my chair with one leg up under the other. I'm wearing jeans that are way too big for me and a sweatshirt that is easily two sizes too big. My hands are curled up inside its sleeves. I try to hide in my clothes. I don't want people to see who I really am. So I let my clothes speak for me. My notebook and pen are on the floor underneath my chair. If I hold them, I will play with them. If I hold them, I might be tempted to write again, and I'm not sure I'm ready to revisit such a painful place.

Not tonight.

Not ever.

I wait.

I glance up under my lids to see if I can catch a glimpse of what the other women are doing.

Maybe they won't be writing either and we can just talk.

I can't see anything.

So I raise my head slightly.

I catch the eye of one of the counselors.

Shit!

"Vanessa, is there a problem? Don't you want to try to write something down?"

I clench my teeth.

Sure.

I reach down and pick up my notebook and pen. I casually flip through what I've written so far. The ink blurs as I pass over the pages to find one that's blank.

I secretly pray there won't be one, that perhaps I've already filled up my notebook and will have to wait until next time.

But I'm not that lucky.

It stares at me, pristine and white. Waiting for my deepest and darkest thoughts.

Halloween, my sixth-grade year. My youth group was having a fall festival. My mother had spent most of the week preparing arts and crafts for it. I'd stayed up late more than once that week helping her make and wrap a sea of popcorn balls, decorate pumpkins, and put together goodie bags. I couldn't wait to go. I had heard about it for weeks and it was finally here!

The night before the party, one of my brothers and I were asked to do the dishes. So we did. The best that a nine- and an eleven-year-old could. By adult standards, it was probably half-assed, but for us, it was a good job.

In retrospect, I have no doubt my parents were tired. So much of their personal time had been taken up by this fall festival at our church, and so to say their tempers and patience were short would be an understatement.

But that wasn't our fault.

"Vanessa! Get back in here and wash one of these dishes. There's still food on it!"

So I did.

Not two minutes later.

"Vanessa, dammit, I told you to wash this dish, now get in here!"

I already did, but I went in and did it again.

This dish was a pan with a coating of baked-on food. I don't remember what we had, probably meatloaf or something, and the pan was completely caked with food. I hadn't gotten it completely out of the corners, and that was the problem.

So I tried it a third time.

This time, I was being watched.

I tried to do it, I really did, but the food just didn't want to come out of the corner. I used a brush, a sponge, a scouring pad, but I just couldn't make it work. So I did the best that I could and put it back on the drainer by the sink.

Not good enough.

"Vanessa, get in here! I will not *have you half-assing your jobs around here. I have worked hard all day long. Your mother has worked hard all day, and now we need your help. Is that too much to ask? You're old enough to start helping out around here and it needs to be done correctly. I've asked you to clean this pan four times now and it is still not clean.*"

But I did clean it.

"Oh, so you call this clean? There's shit all over it. How could you have cleaned it?"

But I did.

Slap!

"Don't talk back to me. I told you to clean this pan and I expect it to be clean. Now run some hot water, put on some gloves, and clean this goddamned pan!"

I started to cry.

"Stop crying, Vanessa. You know better than to half-ass something in this house. It's late. I'm tired. You're tired. Now let's get this cleaned up so we can do something else."

I stood there and scrubbed that pan, but I couldn't make it spotless. It was like the food was melted onto the pan. So I again did the best that I could and turned the pan over so the food wouldn't show.

"Vanessa! That's it. I've had it. We don't ask you to do much around this house, but you have got to learn what is right and wrong. Did you think if you turned the pan over I wouldn't see it? Do you think I'm that stupid?"

No.

"What?"

I didn't say anything.

Slap!

"Now I want you and your brother to stand here and redo these dishes."

All of them?

"Yes, all of them."

But they aren't all dirty.

Slap!

"Don't talk back to me!"

I couldn't do anything but stand there and hold my cheeks. My braces were imbedded in them.

In my mind I cursed out my father, again, and prayed for a bolt of lightning to kill him—instantly. I hated the way he talked to me and the way he made me feel. But I didn't have the courage to say anything, so then I hated myself. For being a coward and a disappointment. Again. Why do I fear my father so much? Why does he seem to hate me so much? Doesn't he see I tried? No. In my house effort counts for nothing. My father is only interested in the end result and the end result, again, is that I have failed.

My brother and I hand washed every dish in that kitchen. Every cabinet was unloaded and cleaned. The dishwasher was unloaded and cleaned. Finally, after about two hours, we were done.

And then the Tupperware came.

In our basement was an entire storage area of Tupperware that my mother had collected.

We hand washed every piece.

Every lid.

Every bowl.

Everything.

At midnight, we finally finished.

"Now, you know how to wash dishes correctly. The next time I ask you to do something, I expect it to be done correctly. Is that understood?"

I nodded.

I was so tired I would have said anything to make him stop talking. I just wanted to go to bed and forget what a horrible day it was. In the back of my mind, I prayed for death. Maybe he'd feel guilty then if his asking me to hand wash every dish in the house was my last task on earth. But then his eyes met mine and I knew what I was asking was impossible. If I died, I'd be an even bigger disappointment, because that would mean I was even weaker than my father believed I was.

"Now, I want you to clean up the sink and get ready for bed. And because you couldn't seem to do this right the first time I asked, you are grounded."

But what about the party?

"You're not going."

But I'm supposed to help.

"I'm sorry. Your mother will take care of whatever you were supposed to do. You will be here thinking about why it is you aren't at the party. Maybe next time you'll do things right without talking back."

I was devastated. I had looked so forward to that party and it was taken away. After washing all of those stupid dishes I still couldn't go.

When I think of that night, all I remember is the pain I put myself through before I fell asleep. I had to be quiet. I could not risk making any noise and so I did what I always did: hit myself in the head until I passed out.

In retrospect, I know my dad was frustrated. I expect that my not being able to wash that dish was the icing on a very tall cake. Maybe he'd had a hard day at work and was powerless to assert himself there. Maybe he and my mother had been fighting and he needed to show what a big man he was. Maybe he couldn't control anything else at that moment, but he could control me and that stupid pan. Or, maybe he was just a bad father. Maybe this was his way of intimidating his kids into submission.

But it didn't work.

Instead of being submissive, I became resourceful. I learned that I could do what I wanted to do as long as no one else knew about it.

I learned to live a lie.

"Is it possible that your father tried to control you because at that moment he felt out of control?"

Yes. But that doesn't make what he did right.

"No, it doesn't. But I want you to think about what *you* do. Do you cut when you feel out of control? Is that *your* last resort?"

Yes.

By the time I have reached the point of cutting, I have exhausted all my other options for feeling in control. My cutting is a way of saying to the world I am hurting, I am out of control, and no one cared enough to help me.

"Do you want someone to stop you?"

I don't know. I know how I feel when I see what I've done to myself. Maybe other people feel the same way. Part of me feels bad and remorseful that I couldn't find any other way to deal with my feelings. It makes me feel weak and desperate. But another part of me feels in control. Powerful. It's like I'm saying to the world, I don't need you to care about me. I can take care of myself. I don't need you to hurt me because I can do it more often and more effectively than you can. It's like I am insulated from the world through my cutting. By putting up a wall, I keep people away and thereby ensure they can't judge or hurt me. In a way, it has become a self-fulfilling prophecy. I want people to reach out, but I am afraid of what they will think of me if I allow myself to be honest and vulnerable with them. So, I make myself inaccessible—indirectly because of my inability to express myself orally and then directly because my scars scare people. They see them, decide helping me will take too much effort, and don't want anything to do with me. Whatever the reason, the end result is the same. I am and feel totally alone most of the time.

"Would you let someone stop you if they tried?"

You mean, stop me from cutting?

"Yes."

No, probably not. By that time, it's too late. The ball has been set in motion. The time for someone to help me or intervene is way before the cutting stage.

"But how are people to know where you are? How do they know when it's almost too late?"

I don't know. Sometimes I don't know. All I know is the signs are there. I can see them; why can't anyone else? I understand if they are too wrapped up in their own lives to pay any attention to mine, but then they should understand why the cuts are there. Their negligence helped to create them. Part of me believes the people in my life bear some responsibility for what I do. If they knew how their decisions affected me, maybe they would be more assertive. Push the issue. Not believe me when I say everything is okay when clearly it isn't.

"Tell me about that."

I think my personality changes a little before I cut. I withdraw. I don't want to talk to anyone. I cry a lot, and sometimes for no reason. I'm short with people; I have no patience. These are all clues. These are signs that should be red flags to people.

"So what does it say when no one recognizes them?"

That they don't care. That I'm not important enough for them to spend their time on. That what happens to me is irrelevant to them. But then a larger part of me believes that I am not worth the effort in the first place. People have busy lives that pull them in a million different directions. Who am I to say that my crisis is any more important than anyone else's? So I'm having a bad day. I should get over it, right? It's not someone else's responsibility to hand hold me through the highs and lows of life. I need to be strong, deal with things on my own. Period.

"So, if someone asked you if you were okay, you would tell them no?"

Probably not.

"Then how are they supposed to know you aren't okay?"

I can't tell them! If I do, then I am weak and needy. I am supposed to be strong and resilient. Other people count on me to be there for them. If I say I need them to be there for me, what does that say?

"It says you're human."

No, it doesn't. It says I can't do it on my own. I've *always* done things on my own.

"So, how is this different?"

I don't know, but it is. I'm not like other people. I never have been. Some people get mad, scream and yell and it's over with. I just bottle that up inside. I can't let people know what I'm feeling because feelings aren't acceptable, right? I've never had someone sit me down and say, "Why are you so angry, Vanessa? Do you want to talk about it?" That's never happened. Why? Because I think that people are afraid to ask—afraid they won't know how to make things better. If there is never an acknowledgment of a problem, a person can't be held responsible for not doing anything to make it better, right? The bottom line is I'm not supposed to be angry or frustrated or jealous or depressed. If I am, then I have to deal with it on my own. So I do. I cut myself and that too is unacceptable.

"So what's the answer?"

I don't know. That's why I came to see you.

"What are you most afraid of?"

Dying.

Breaking my arms.

Stabbing myself in the thighs.

Hanging myself from a bar in the closet.

Wanting the pain in my heart to end so badly that I do something that will forever change who I am.

I don't want to die until I know who that is—who I am.

"Where do you think your eating disorder fits into this? Do you not realize that your starving yourself could also lead to your death?"

Sacrifice is noble. I learned a long time ago to give up food and then tell myself I didn't want it anyway.

"Was there a big event in your life that prompted you to start denying yourself food?"

I was already aware of foods and had been labeling them in my mind as good or bad ever since my mother became diabetic. But when I said "no, thank you" to food at that time, it was a choice. There was plenty of food in the house, so if there was a feeling of wanting, it was because I'd put myself in a position of denial. In high school, my father left us in a crippling financial bind. I don't ever remember my mother monitoring what my brothers and I ate as much as she did in the months after my father left. We were told to cut back on how much we ate so the food would last between pay-checks. But with three growing kids, it wasn't always enough. I was the oldest. I knew my mother couldn't cut back and my brothers were growing, so I decided to be the one to do without. If I am able to do without something that everyone else around me needs, then I am stronger than they are. If I can say "no, thank you" to things, even things I desperately want, then I am disciplined. I learned how disci-plined I really was between the ages of 13 and 17. My mother's mother would send us boxes of food in the mail. I can remember getting those boxes, seeing my mother's face as she opened them, and having mixed emotions. One, I was glad for the boxes because having food in the house took some pressure off my mother. There would usually be some sort of treat in the boxes like cookies or sugar cereal or something that we wouldn't have been able to buy otherwise and my brothers would be so excited for those things. But I was so angry at my father for putting us in that position. And I was so embarrassed that things were so desperate that we needed to have food sent to us that it killed whatever appetite I might have had. If I didn't eat the food from the boxes, then my mother and brothers could have more and I wanted them to. I don't remember ever even debating that issue. The second the boxes arrived, I remember knowing in my heart I wasn't going to eat any. I believed my father had left because of me and felt that by giving up my portion of the food in the boxes, I was doing what I could to make up for that fact.

"So how does that event contribute to your behavior now?"

I guess part of me feels like I've gone without for so long that to finally say yes would be a tremendous sign of weakness. As I got older, I learned if I am a size zero when everyone around me isn't, then I am noticed. The more attention I bring to myself, the less I want to disappoint those around me. It's like a vicious cycle. It took discipline to get me where I am. For me to gain weight would show a lack of discipline and I can't let that happen.

"The last time you were here, Vanessa, you mentioned that you'd learned to live a lie. I want you to tell me more about that."

My mother would tell you I have had a strong will since the day I was born. I have had goals and have always seemed to know how to reach them. I don't need people to motivate me or get me on track. It's like I've been on track my entire life. That has been a big problem because sometimes what I want to do and what other people want me to do aren't the same thing. Sometimes my priorities aren't the same as everybody else's.

"And that is a problem?"

Apparently so. I think most of the time I got into trouble at home was because I was trying to assert my will at a time that wasn't "convenient."

"What do you mean by that?"

Think about it. You have a stay-at-home mom and three kids. In order for my mom to have some sort of order or sanity, she needed all of her kids to be on the same page most of the time.

"And?"

Well, even though I understand that, it doesn't mean it will happen. What works for other people doesn't always work for me. I hate being pigeonholed. I hate feeling like what I want isn't important. So, I verbalized that frustration and most of the time it wasn't well received.

"What would happen?"

When I was little, I had to stand in the corner or go to my room without my books or toys. But what my parents didn't seem to understand was that their punishment didn't stop my will. If I was sent to my room with no books or toys, so what? I had my imagination. I could escape in my mind and still be doing something other than what they wanted me to be doing, which was thinking about why I was being punished. It was very powerful. I created a whole other world for myself and could visit it whenever I wanted.

As I got older, if I got punished, I would find ways to make my punishment work to my advantage. Sent to my room with no supper? Great! Now I had time to clean my room or write in my diary. You want to take my books away? That's fine. I have paper and pen somewhere in my room that I can use to write my *own* stories. Send me to bed early? Fantastic! Now I have a chance to look through books with a penlight or to sit up in my bed and practice teaching to my stuffed animals. I took great pride in knowing that I was doing what I wanted to do, not what someone else told me to do.

"Why does that bother you so much that other people tell you what to do?"

Because I think they underestimate my abilities. I am more mature than most people, always have been. I don't need that outside control. I can control myself. I don't need someone to structure my day. I can do that just fine. I have never had a problem with time management or motivation. I have always wanted people to just step back and watch. See what I can do and be amazed.

"You need that attention?"

Yes.

I want people to realize that they are in the presence of an anomaly. I don't say greatness because that's arrogant. But I will say an anomaly. I am a rarity. And I don't think most people know how to react to me.

"So how does all of this fit in with you living a lie?"

The first part of that is doing what I want to do, regardless of what other people think I'm doing. But the second part of that comes from feelings. Feelings were not welcome in my house unless they were joyful. If you were angry, you were sent to your room until you could get yourself back under control. If you were sad, you'd better get over it, because the expectation was that once my father got home, everything was June Cleaver perfect. The house was clean. We were clean. And everyone was getting along. Even if you weren't. You were expected to put on your game face and cover it up. We were told as children that my dad worked too hard to come home to an unhappy house. He needed us to be happy and upbeat. So we were. Even if it was a lie most of the time.

"You don't think he knew?"

I don't know. Maybe he did, maybe he didn't. But he bought into it, regardless. There was no "tell me about it" in my house. There were no raised voices, slamming of doors, or venting of frustration unless you were my father. He was the only one who seemed to be exempt from most of the rules of the house. Quite convenient, I've always thought.

"What do you mean?"

He could be mad at you, but you couldn't be mad back. It was like you didn't have that privilege. He could call you names, make you feel bad, and smack you around and you had to take it. There was no standing up for yourself, because if you did, you were slapped. So, you learned to say things behind people's backs. You learned to say things in the sanctity of your room, quietly, where only you could hear. You learned to say things in the dark. If you were so mad you could hit something, you held it in, because the second you did so and my mother or father heard you, then *you* were the one in trouble. So, there again, you learned to hit things after the fact. Quietly. In the dark. Then you could have whatever feelings you wanted and no one else had to be troubled with them.

"So what did that teach you about feelings?"

That they were inappropriate. That they were something to be hidden and ignored. It's funny. If I had to sum up my life in one sentence, I think it would be: What were you thinking?

"Why was that a problem?"

Because most of the time my feelings were so strong I couldn't hide them or ignore them. And there isn't always a reason for feelings. That's what makes them feelings. They aren't rational.

"So what happened when you did reveal your feelings?"

I got into trouble. If I was mad at my brothers, I would say something. I would tell them they were stupid or that I was mad at them, and then before I knew it, *I* was the one in trouble for saying hateful things. Forget whatever my brothers had done to piss me off in the first place. No! They could do whatever, but the second I responded to it, I was in trouble. So I learned to keep it inside. I learned to let my feelings build up until I exploded. Then, if I got into trouble, I was so overwhelmed with the feelings that I'd been harboring, it didn't seem to matter much.

"Tell me about your feelings. You've said you couldn't express them as a child and don't feel equipped to express them as an adult. Do you feel bad about the feelings you have?"

I feel tremendous guilt over the feelings I have. It's like I never feel the right feeling. If I laugh at the *wrong* time, I'm insensitive. If I don't laugh at the *right* time, I have no sense of humor. If I'm angry, it never seems to be at the right level; it's too much or too little for the situation. If I'm happy, it may or may not be justified. Somewhere along the way I learned to second-guess myself. For example, as a teenager, if I had the chance to go out and eat with a friend, I would feel bad because I knew that my family wasn't going to be able to eat that food with me. So I ate less to take away my guilt. I didn't enjoy it. As an adult, if I have the chance to travel, I feel bad about it because I know my mother loves to travel and rarely has the opportunity. I feel selfish by not sharing what I have with those who don't have the same things. So, it's like no matter what, the experience is tainted. If I enjoy it, I'm selfish. If I don't enjoy it because of the guilt I feel, I'm a thankless person who doesn't deserve that opportunity. I would love, for once in my life, to not feel guilty.

"Where do all of your feelings go?"

Into making the bruises and scars that riddle my body. I've had to be careful. As a child, had my parents found out what I was doing, they would have punished me even more. I honestly believe I would have been spanked for just trying to cope. And so I hid what I did. Even now, I can close my eyes and hear the sole of the shoe like a cobbler's hammer on my arm. A rhythmic *whack! whack! whack!* as the capillaries in my wrist, forearm, and elbow joint ruptured. If I was going to hurt, then I was going to hurt *my* way. Then, in the midst of the pain, if someone were to ask me what I was thinking, I could honestly say nothing. If I hurt bad enough, I didn't have to think at all.

"What about now?"

The same thing. When I look at the scars on my body, I see a variety of emotions: anger, fear, frustration, and guilt. Guilt over hurting people's feelings. Guilt over not being strong enough to set personal boundaries. Guilt over pushing people away. Guilt over needing people in the first place. Guilt over dreams unfulfilled. Guilt over the brazenness to dream at all. In one word, I feel bad. Bad that I can't be the person I think others think I am and want me to be. I feel bad because most of the time I choose to make other people happy over myself. I feel bad because I am not who I know I can be and that frustrates me.

"So, do you think you are living a lie?"

Absolutely. As a young person, I was able to put on a game face because most of the time I dealt with my feelings in the dark. I had punched myself until I couldn't feel it anymore, or I'd ripped a toenail off to the quick, or I'd hit myself in the head until I passed out. I did those things because they were quiet and no one had to know. Instead of other people saying things that made me feel bad, I could do it myself. Instead of other people spanking me for something I'd done, I could do it myself. My own way. In my own time.

Now, as an adult, I still don't deal with my feelings because I'm not supposed to have them, right? And I am surrounded by people who seem to have an agenda for my life. So, over the years, I have learned to navigate this road and almost split myself between what others want and what I want for myself.

"Isn't that a lot of work?"

Yes. I'm exhausted most of the time. But I don't see any way around it.

"Give me an example of what you mean about splitting yourself."

Any time I have to say something is okay when I don't think it is, I've split myself. Any time I do something I don't want to do, I split myself. What's happened is that over time I've lost sense of who I really am. I *really* feel like I am two people. I feel like the person people know is the one they have helped to create. But the person I *really* am is someone no one knows anything about. She's ambitious, highly creative, and scared to death. I think if people knew about this part of me they would reject me, and so I keep it to myself.

For example, I became a teacher because I admired my father and my own teachers so much. Short of my parents, teachers influenced my life more than anyone else. I knew my teachers **loved me** through their words and actions every day. A big part of me believes I am alive because of my teachers and their interest in who I was and what I was going through at the time. They were my safe place. I want to be that for someone else. I want to reach out to those kids who don't have a stable home life or who feel lost. I want to develop a personal relationship with my students so I can encourage them in the goals they have set for themselves. But as our nation's schools focus more and more on test scores, this kind of relationship is deemed unimportant. I disagree. I want my students to know *who* they are, *where* they come from, and *what* they want to do with their life. I am continually told I cannot save them all. But I want to. I don't want to give up on *any* of my students, regardless of whether or not they come regularly or pass my class. So, here is one way in which I split myself. I do as much for them as I can academically (which the school believes is important) and then I do what *I* think is important, which is to show my students that someone cares for them and believes in them no matter what (what *I* think is important). Most of my peers think this is ridiculous; that establishing a relationship with my kids is a waste of time and energy. In order to have a good working environment, I have to split myself here again. I am nice to these teachers. I listen to what they have to say and smile and nod. Then I go into my classroom and do what *I* want to do. My students and I are better for it.

I stand in front of my students each day with a smile on my face, regardless of how I feel on the inside. My students come to me asking for advice on many of life's issues because they believe I have all the answers. Even when I assure them I don't, they believe otherwise. What if they knew who their teacher really was? What if they found out how I cope with the feelings on the inside so I can put a smile on the outside? Would they tell me how thin I am if they knew I was starving myself? Keeping these parts of myself private has allowed me to keep my job. But they have also contributed to a huge division in my sense of self. I have to wonder which part of me is real? Will it ever be possible to merge these two facets and love who that is? Can I have low self-esteem, an eating disorder, be a cutter, but also be a highly accomplished and well-loved educator? Is it possible for people in my life to see through the facade I have created for myself and appreciate who is standing on the other side?

"Do you do this with everything?"

Yes.

My marriage.

My family.

Myself.

"Tell me about that."

There are some things that my husband really believes in and puts emphasis on.

"Like what?"

Like family time. If I see my mom and stepfather twice a year, I'm fine with that. I can't spend too much time with my family because of the dysfunction that exists there. But for him, if he doesn't see his family once or twice a *week*, it's a big deal. If I fight this, it causes a rift in our marriage, so I don't. I go along with it and act like it's equally important to me in order to keep the peace.

"What would happen if you didn't do that?"

Probably nothing. But at some level there would be this major divide between us and over time it would be an issue. His parents would start to ask why I never come over and if they've done something wrong. It's just not worth it. It's easier to just go with the flow than to fight it.

"So how do you know what things to go with the flow on and which ones to fight?"

I guess my heart tells me. I've been in situations before where I've been asked to do things that went against my belief system, and so I left. I either quit the job or did something about it. And then there are other things that are more of a nuisance than they are major problems, and so I just kind of resign myself to giving in on those. But in my heart I recognize that that is a choice I'm making, that it's not because someone is behind me browbeating me into submission.

"Why do you think other people want you to be submissive?"

Because then I'm easier to control. I know my parents wanted me to submit to their will, and the fact that I rarely would was a real problem.

Once while coloring in a book, I remember someone telling me to color the sky blue. I looked up at them, picked up a purple crayon, and went to town. My whole life is like that. I don't know why. It's not like I didn't think the sky would look nice in blue, but because I wasn't the one who thought of coloring it blue, I didn't want to give another person the satisfaction of telling me what to do, and so I chose a different color. Had *I* been the one to pick blue, it would have been perfect!

"I'm confused. It seems like as a child you wanted to please your parents by doing what they asked. But you've just told me that there were times when you purposefully went against their wishes. Can you explain that?"

I think after a certain point in my life, probably age 4 or so (coincidentally that is the earliest I can remember self-injuring), I figured out that no matter what I did, on some level I would be a disappointment to my parents. I worked hard at being a good daughter and tried to do my best, but more often than not, my best wasn't good enough. I wasn't acting my age or I wasn't being responsible or I wasn't being thoughtful of others. I wasn't listening or doing things fast enough. It was always something. So on the one hand, yes, I did try hard to do what was asked of me. But on the other hand, if my parents' request was one I perceived as a suggestion (like the coloring incident), then I believed I had the choice about how it was done.

"**Role models** are very important to us. They allow us to see elements of ourselves in new ways. They provide for us a road map to the kind of person we want to become. Each of you sitting in this room is a product of the role models you've had in your life. For some people, their repeated exposure to negative role models has contributed to low self-esteem and negative behaviors. For others, positive role models have given you a sense of hope that one day your lives would be different, meaningful. Tonight we're going to talk about the very first role models you ever had, your parents. I want you to think about your relationship with them and see if you can't identify where you get some of your tendencies from. This doesn't mean it's your parent's fault that you are the way that you are. However, each of you adopted behavior patterns from somewhere and if we can identify where these patterns come from, it will allow you to see that there are other patterns that you can choose to adopt as well."

———————

This will be an easy one. Parent number one, my mother. My mother and I have a love/hate relationship. From the very beginning of my life, I have known that she and I were totally different. She is highly skilled with her hands, I with my mind. She knows how to cook from scratch; I prefer recipes from a box. She knows how to sew clothes by hand; I know how to bargain shop. She always wanted to be a mother; I never even wanted to get married. So, our communication was limited. The things she valued and thought were important, I dismissed as trivial and insignificant. I loved her for being a mother, but I hated to think that I would have a life like hers. She was the nurturing parent. She was the one who met me at the door each day after school and took care of me when I was sick. She was the one I could talk to and ask questions of. In many ways, she was exactly the kind of mother I would want to be if I had kids. On the other hand, I resented the hell out of her for not defending me in the presence of my father. More than once I could hear her say, as I was being spanked, "Jim, that's enough," and my father would tell her to butt out. Rather than interfere, she would leave. I hated her for that. Part of me still does.

Parent number two, my father. He and I have more of a hate than a love relationship. He is a perfectionist, a mental giant, a leader in the community. He epitomized most of what I thought I wanted to become in life. He had a solid education, a great career, and a wonderful family. But his need for accolades forced him to work a tremendous amount of hours and left him with little emotional energy to give his family. My father is not an emotional man. He's a fix-it man. He doesn't want to hear your problems; he wants to know what they are, in a nutshell, so he can fix them—quickly. And so he can move on to something else of greater importance. My father was abusive. With a temper shorter than a TNT fuse, you never knew what to expect when you were around him. He could turn on a dime. You learned quickly to walk on eggshells around him, lest you set him off. But because he was so smart and good at so many things, that part of his personality seemed to be tolerated.

On the other hand, my dad was good at making me feel special. Once a year or so, he and I would have a "date." We would go to a downtown hotel, dressed in our Sunday best, and share a banana split and ride the glass elevators. He took me to see my first theatrical performance. My first orchestra performance. My first museum lecture. My father impressed upon me a need for culture, good manners, and to carry oneself with an air of distinction. He was an enigma to me. I wanted to make him proud; his opinion of me mattered so much, yet I have wished him dead for most of my life. My father's wit is quicker than his temper, and he could reduce you to tears at the drop of a hat. When I think of my father, the "I love yous" are few and far between. But the biting comments—"You are so retarded the Special Olympics wouldn't even take you," "You are a fucking vulture," and when I first started having an issue with eating, "What are you, a third-world wannabe?"—are permanently imprinted on my memory.

I never figured out how to make my father happy. If I got an A minus on a report card, I was asked why it wasn't an A. If I got a 95 on a test, I was asked why it wasn't a 100. I wasn't athletic. I wasn't as musically gifted as my brothers were, and I could never make myself shine in his presence. One day, I vowed I would do something so wonderful with my life that he would realize what he had passed over for most of my life. But more often than not, I think I have spent my life out of his favor; without his blessing.

When I cut, usually it is his voice I hear telling me I am worthless, stupid, and a disappointment. In a sick way, I think it would give him pride to know this. It would mean that his impact on me has been greater than I would like to believe, and certainly would hate to admit. At other times, the voice is my own. It speaks to all the insecurities I possess with regard to my marriage, intellect, weight, self-esteem, and effectiveness as a teacher. On my worst days, I hear both voices. That's when I feel the most helpless. Between the two voices, I feel like a failure. With my father's voice, I was a disappointment as a child. With my voice, I am a disappointment as an adult. That's all there is, right? There isn't another stage of life when I can redeem myself. I feel like I spend every waking moment trying to silence that inner adult voice. If I can do that, regardless of how many battle scars I get in the process, then it will be worth it.

I finally got my own room when I was nine years old. For most people, the room itself would have been a private sanctuary. But not for me. In my room I felt vulnerable, like I was being watched. And so I found my own sanctuary in the back of my closet.

If I moved my shoe rack out and slid the door closed, I had a space that fit my little body perfectly. There, I could sit knees under chin and hold myself. Assure myself that I was still alive and that nothing would last forever. There, I could cry and ask God to take me away. There, I could let the darkness envelop me and comfort me in a way the light never has.

My closet space was a tremendous secret. No one would have understood it or supported my going there. So, there was an element of fear in my closet. I knew if the door to my room was closed, there would never be a knock, just a sudden opening and then a yell wondering where I was. I could never let my hiding place be known, and so more often then not, I sat there, rocking, crying, praying, and listening for telltale footsteps, heavy breathing, or any sound that might be a signal for me to get out and return my shoe rack to its place.

As I got older, the closet became even more important to me. It was a place where I could sit, still knees under chin, and cry over the wounds I'd made on *my body, or the food I wanted but would not allow myself to eat. I believed God was in that dark place, and I relished every moment I spent there.*

In the dark, I never had to see any of my physical awkwardness or deficiencies. In the dark, I was perfect. I was loved. I was safe.

I continued to have "closet time" through my first years of marriage. But by then, I was secure enough in my life and the people in it that I could take a pillow and blanket in there and fall asleep. No longer forced to sit up knees to chin, I had a chance to fully lie out and let the dark embrace me completely. No one could hurt me there. No harsh words. No physical pain. No feelings of disappointment.

It was, and still is, my favorite room in the house.

Over time, I feel like my mind became my closet. The more the outside world tried to hurt me, the more I retreated into a safe place. I physically escaped when I could, but there wasn't always time to do that. So again, I split. I created a part of myself whose only job is to hide me and nurture me through the situation.

I can't believe I'm saying this out loud! I can't even look at my therapist. *Reproach or reassurance is too great a risk to even attempt eye contact. I stare straight ahead and talk to a picture hanging on the opposite wall.*

To try to explain this to anyone, even to write it down, makes me feel crazy. Does this mean I cannot cope? Does this mean I can't handle things?

"What do *you* think it means?"

I wait. I feel like a scab has been ripped off part of my soul. My closet time is sacred. I don't know how much further I want to discuss this. I don't want it to be tainted by overanalysis or subjectivity.

I think my therapist senses my hesitancy and pauses before proceeding.

"Vanessa, I want you to tell me more about your closet time. What did you feel when you were in there?"

Safe.

Absolutely, without a doubt, safe.

Most of the time I felt cold. Not the same cold as I've told you I feel before I cut. No, this cold was different. This was like being naked in a snowstorm. I would physically shiver, and so I got into the habit of bringing a blanket in with me.

"What made you cold?"

I don't know. It was the same type of feeling you get when you are thinking about something and you shiver. That bone-shaking, deep-down cold feeling. Maybe it's because I knew how hard things would be for me if I were caught. Or perhaps the pressure to escape was stronger than the adrenaline coursing through my veins.

But as a child, I believed it was the presence of God or angels, because I never had that sensation at any other time.

"Why would God make you feel that way?"

Maybe I just wanted to believe in Him so badly. I *begged* for a sign that He was there, that He could see me, and that He knew I needed help. *So* many times I prayed for Him to rescue me, to take me away—that if He weren't going to take my father, then kill me. The pain was too much. It was like dying a slow and painful death and no one knew it. But I wanted to believe that God knew it and that He felt pity for me and would save me. As a child, another part of me feared God. If my biological father wasn't pleased with me, I realized that God might also be mad at me for not being a better person. Perhaps guilt was His way of letting me know that He too was disappointed. And so I started trying to apologize to God—to show Him that I really was a good person and that He could trust me to fulfill my purpose in life. Sometimes my conversations with Him were honest, heartfelt confessions of my dreams and desires. At other times, they consisted of me crying and begging God to let my dreams come true because I was worth it.

I found that if I focused hard enough on God and really threw myself into talking to Him, most of my inhibitions and outside layers were stripped away. There, in the dark and quiet of my closet, I allowed myself to be vulnerable. I felt emotionally naked, and I wanted to think He responded to that. By making me feel cold, He let me know He was there.

"Did this comfort you?"

Yes.

I have felt so alone for most of my life. I don't think anyone understands me, or the pressure I feel like I'm under most of the time, and so yes, I did feel comfort. I still do.

"Are there other ways that you've been able to feel like you're not alone?"

Rarely. Every once in a while, something will happen that will totally be a God thing. It's not a coincidence; it's from God. But those things don't happen every day. It's hard to feel His presence when you feel so isolated most of the time. It's like I'm a phantom—a shadow that just drifts through life and no one even knows I'm there. But when I'm hurting, *I* know I'm there.

"So what do you consider a God thing?"

Anything that happens that is so far-fetched that it seems impossible. Like, for example, last year I was begging God for a sign that I should stay in teaching. I wasn't feeling like I was effective, and I desperately needed a sign to let me know whether I should stay where I was or to start looking elsewhere. I had this internal war going on for months, and the week I decided that I should quit and do something else, I was given a national excellence in teaching award. That award came at the precise time that I needed an answer. In reality, that award could have come at any time. People in my school had been getting them at intervals for weeks, but not me. When I needed it the most, it finally came. That was my sign.

About five years ago, I was at work and there was this sense that I needed to go home. It was the end of the day, but I had planned on working late. I tried to do some work, but all the phone calls I tried to make ended in a busy signal. I tried to do paperwork and my pen was out of ink. I ended up going home and walked in on a ringing phone. My husband's mother had lapsed into a diabetic coma and the hospital was trying to reach her children. Had I not gone home, I would have missed that call. There has never been another day when so many things inhibited my ability to do my job. I don't know where that urgency came from. It had to be a God thing.

Or this . . . this is a true God thing. I had to have emergency surgery when I was in graduate school. This was a tremendous financial burden on my husband and me. I dreaded getting the bills because I didn't see how we could pay them. We could hardly keep our heads above water as it was. A couple months later, the bills started to arrive and so I went to the hospital's financial office to make payment arrangements. I waited and waited for someone to help me, and I prayed. I asked God for a nice financial officer, someone who would be sensitive to my plight and would give me a plan that was doable. When the lady finally came out, I told her my situation about my husband and I being in school and she looks up and says, "I know. All of your bills have been dismissed. The hospital chooses patients each year to forgive bills for, and your bills have been forgiven. You have a zero balance." *That* is a God thing. I have never heard of a hospital doing something like that, but it happened. *God* made that happen.

And, I guess, in the whole scheme of things, I am living proof of a God thing. I should be dead by now. Goodness knows I haven't taken care of the body I was given. I haven't been the child my parents deserved and, in many ways, I have lived a life of selfishness. People more deserving of life are dead, yet I am still here.

"So if God can make good things happen for you, why do you think He's allowed you to go through some of the negative things?"

I guess to make me stronger; I don't know. I feel like, for the most part, I've been one of God's greatest disappointments. I haven't taken care of the body He gave me. I don't respect my parents the way I'm supposed to. I long to be something that I know I can't be—perfect—and so it just seems like no matter what good things come up in my life, I miss them because I feel like I'm not living up to His expectations.

"Do you *really* feel this way?"

Yes.

Of all the parents in the world, God chose my parents for me. For them, to my father especially, I am a disappointment. If I am such a disappointment to my earthly father, how can I not be a disappointment to my heavenly father as well?

"What if I told you your biological father isn't perfect? That he made mistakes? That he, too, is a product of his past?"

In my mind I know that. But I want to hear him say that he is proud of me and the things I've done with my life. I don't want to keep feeling like I'm stupid next to him and worthless. He helped to make me. His blood flows through my veins. Isn't there something about me he could be proud of? Even when I totally screwed up? I don't think he believes so.

"Do you need him to love you in order for you to love yourself?"

Maybe, maybe not. I don't want to need his approval, but I do. Part of me says to hell with him. Let him go on in his splendid ignorance. But the other part of me wants his blessing. I want to know he realizes that *I* am one of his greatest accomplishments in life. I want him to acknowledge and be happy with me.

The first time I was sick and away from home happened when I was fifteen years old. I was a counselor at a weeklong church camp. I had waited and waited for this week to arrive, and when it did, I finally felt like I was on my way to being an adult. This was the first time I would be in charge of my own group of girls age 8 to 12. I was the one who was supposed to make sure they woke up on time each day, made all of their craft sessions, led the nature hikes, escorted them to meals, and enforced the lights-out rule each night. I was an adult in every sense of the word.

But on the third day of camp, my body started to break down. Perhaps it was my strict dieting that finally caught up with me; perhaps it was my body's reaction to the parasites that lived in the water at the camp. Whatever it was left me with a high fever, diarrhea, and complete dehydration. One night after campfire, I passed out on the beach. I was completely humiliated and felt that, once again, my body had betrayed me. I had my eyes on one of the male counselors and I didn't want him to think I was sickly. When I woke up to him wiping my face with ocean water, I about died. One minute we were holding hands, talking, the next I was lying in the sand. I was taken out of my cabin and placed in the nurse's cabin, totally isolated from any of the other campers and staff. I was given ginger ale and placed in a quiet, dark room. I cried. I cried for being weak; I cried for being sick. I cried for being away from home and wanting my mother to take care of me.

That week changed me forever. First, the boy I had my eyes on gave me my first kiss. It was nothing like what I thought a kiss would be and I giggled through it. But a kiss is a kiss, and I felt a part of my soul mature that day. And second, it was the first time I had ever been away from home and sick. It was the first time my mother hadn't been there to take care of me when I needed her, and it left me feeling hollow inside. Forget being an adult; I wanted to go home. I wanted my mother to hug me and to fix me soup and run me a warm bath. I wanted someone to feel sorry for me and dote on me the way only a mother can. But no one did. I was alone. In the dark, again, and completely alone.

At some point, someone brought me my luggage so I could brush my teeth and change my clothes. That night, I was returned to my cabin but made to sleep apart from the girls. I stayed for two more days before one of the other counselors finally took me home.

No one knew I was coming home early, and so once I got there, the house was locked up tight. I had no keys, as I hadn't thought to bring them with me.

And so I waited on the front porch for over an hour. Quietly hurting and desperately wanting someone to find me and make me feel better.

But a large part of my childhood self died that week. I realized that there *would come a time in my life when I would be alone and would have to take care of myself, and that time had come.*

That week changed the way I saw myself in the world. I learned that I was the one who needed to take care of me, and it made me sad.

———————

"But you had been taking care of yourself for so long. Why was this any different?"

Because I guess the other caretaking behaviors were a choice. I made the messes and I cleaned them up. But when you get sick, that isn't something you control. It just happens. From your earliest days, you learn to tell your mother when you don't feel well, and something inside of her jumps into action and she makes you feel better. It's a look. A touch. A cold cloth on your forehead. It's all of those little mommy touches that you just can't do for yourself. It's not the same.

"But isn't that a big part of growing up? Becoming an adult?"

I guess so. But as much as I thought I wanted to be an adult, that weekend showed me I really didn't. I wanted to be seen as responsible and independent, but a small part of me still wanted to be scooped up and held.

"So why didn't you tell your mother that when she came home?"

Because it sounded silly. It still does. I was fifteen years old. I was thinking about boys and college and becoming my own person. For me to admit to her that I still needed her in that way was like taking a huge step backward.

"What do you think she would have said or done had you told her you needed her then?"

Back then, I thought she would have brushed it off, told me to grow up and act like an adult. But now, I really think she would have comforted me. I think part of her would have been glad to know that I still needed her. I had made such an effort to separate myself from her that I think she was feeling sad too. I mean, I didn't need her as a mother anymore, and so our relationship was being redefined. I think she would have welcomed one last chance to "mommy" me a little bit. For old times' sake.

———————

"What are you most afraid of, Vanessa?"

Being a failure.

Being at the end of my life and realizing that I didn't do anything magnificent with it. Dying, and having no one even know I was here.

"There are millions of people in the world, Vanessa. Each of those people did something with their lives. They were parents. Workers. Leaders in their communities. But not all of them will be recognized on a major level when they die."

Maybe they don't care to be recognized, but I do! I want the world to know that Vanessa Vega was here, and that she did something to make the world a better place. I want people to know that I was generous with my time and money, and that I tried to be a friend to people who had no other friends. I don't want to be a byline in an obituary section. I want to be someone who will be missed enough to get the big spread with the picture and a nice write-up. I don't want to just disappear.

"You have mentioned disappearing more than once, Vanessa. What does that mean to you?"

Think of how many people you interact with on a daily basis. At the grocery store. Dry cleaners. Gas station. Bank. How many of those people's names do you know? How many of those people greet *you* by name? Most of them just say hi and move on. You drift in and out of their lives like a shadow, and that's it. I don't want it to be like that. I want to have an interaction with someone and have them know I was there. I don't want to be a number. If I die, I want people to be sad. To miss me *and* the impact I made on the world.

"So, how do you plan on doing this?"

I don't know. On a small level, I think I do have that kind of impact. Most people at work know my name and think I do a good job. People in my housing complex know me and greet me by name. I try to establish a first-name-basis relationship with people at my bank and at businesses I frequent, but that seems really small. I want to do something larger, so that people outside my little ecosystem will know who I am. I want to inspire people to be more, to *do* more, and the only way I can accomplish that is to do something amazing. I believe one person really can change the world. Most people aren't interested in or up to the challenge. But I am! I just want the chance to prove I'm not the disappointment I've felt like most of my life. I want to show the world that its faith in me wasn't misguided. That I did have a good heart and a giving spirit, regardless of what people may think sometimes.

It's funny. I read things like *People* magazine because those are the people most recognized in our society, in our world. I want to see what they are doing, and to try to see how it is that they have made such a name for themselves. Perhaps I live vicariously through them as I flip through the pages. I don't know. Part of me wants to be famous like that. I want to feel like I've lived a life of substance; that I've made a difference.

"But what if you don't? There are millions of people in this world and only a handful of them show up in your magazines. Does that mean that *they* are the only ones who are important?"

No.

But people know who they are. I want people to know who I am, too. I want to feel special enough to have people want to know more about me. I want to be a role model to other people. I want to be significant enough to others that no matter what I do I won't disappear; I won't be invisible.

"Why do you feel invisible?"

I truly believe that if I didn't talk, I could drift through my day without anyone missing me. If I died and didn't show up for work one day, people's first concern would be to replace me. I'm expendable. But if I do something amazing, then perhaps that won't be the case. Perhaps there will be a vested interest in trying to find out what happened. As it is now, who would care? My family? My small circle of friends? That's it.

"So?"

So? The more people know about you, the more people love you. I want to be loved like that. I want people to adore me in that way. If I'm hurting, I want people to want to help me. If I'm in trouble, I want to know there are people around who will help me. As it is now, no one knows anything about me. I could walk off the face of the earth and no one would care. I want to mean more than that. People say, "Oh, *who* you are is totally different from *what* you do." Bullshit. You *are* what you do. If I don't do anything extraordinary with my life, then I am *not* an extraordinary person. If I do something wonderful, then people will like me. Then, I'll be wonderful too.

"What difference does it make?"

It means the difference between life and death for me as a person. I can't imagine that I was brought into this world to live a mediocre life. I need to be more than that. Otherwise, I'm what I've always felt I was: worthless and stupid. I can't believe that's true. But it isn't enough for me to believe it. Other people have to know it isn't true either. And the only way for them to know that is to do something *amazing*.

"I think one of the things you are failing to see here is that who you are has very little to do with what you do. It sounds trite, but you are amazing because of your desire to help other people. You are amazing because of the lengths you'll go to help your students to find success. You are amazing because of the friend you are to those in need. That's enough. Your accomplishments, regardless of how famous they may make you initially, will fade over time. What will remain is the person behind those deeds. You can't negate that fact because it doesn't fit into your idea of *amazing*. Can it not be enough that Vanessa is amazing as a person? Can you accept the fact that if you *never* did another thing, won another award, or received glowing accolades from others you would still be worthy of love?"

No. I can't accept that. And you know why? Because it sounds like a consolation prize. It sounds like if I quit now, I've lost the momentum I need to make my life mean something—not just to others, but to myself. How can I be sure that I've fulfilled my purpose if I don't even know who I really am? It would be the same as me going in to get clothes from a dry cleaner and them asking my name, saying I don't know, and then just getting some clothes off the rack. Maybe they are right for me, maybe they aren't. Wouldn't it be easier to know the name of the person's clothes I was wearing so I could be sure the clothes fit? That's what I need to know. I need to know *who*

Vanessa is, not who the world or my family wants her to be, but who she *really* is, so I know that I am doing all that I am called to do in the short time I have on this earth. I don't care what anyone says. I believe I am called to do something amazing . . . something life changing . . . but I need to find out more about myself first.

"So what do you think is holding you back from knowing that information?"

I don't know. That's what I'm trying to find out.

"**So far,** we've talked about anger, punishment, and control. Tonight, I want us to talk about forgiveness. Now this is a huge topic. So huge, in fact, that we are going to spend more than one group session talking about it. Because when it comes to forgiveness, there are issues of motivation that we need to discuss, such as: Why do I need to forgive this person? Is it necessary for the betterment of the relationship? What will I gain through forgiving this person? Is their trespass against me something my heart can look past? This is an important question, because sometimes the answer is no. This is something you have to decide for yourself. If the answer is no, then the relationship is damaged. But if the answer is yes, then we need to look at the act of forgiveness itself: Do you approach these people and tell them they're forgiven, or do you just do it for yourself? There is power in forgiveness because all the bitterness, resentment, and anger that you may have toward that other person is no longer a part of your spirit. Think about it. When someone hurts you, how many times does that person realize the full extent of what he or she has done? Knowing this person has forgotten about an incident that hurt you in some way leaves you with additional anger and frustration. You aren't hurting the other person by carrying around these feelings, you are only hurting yourself. So, in order to free up that emotional energy for something else, you have to let go of what the person did to you. Done. It's over. Ancient history.

"For each of you, this is a problem. There are individuals in your lives who have hurt you so badly that you've carried around that pain inside of you for years. The results have been emotionally and physically devastating. There are two aspects of forgiveness that we are going to talk about: forgiveness of others and forgiveness of self.

Now, the whole idea of forgiving yourself is intimidating, so we're going to start with something a little less so, which is forgiving someone else. Each of you has someone, or perhaps many people, in your lives who have hurt you. Tonight, I am asking you to pick one of them. I want you to focus on *only* that person for this exercise. Okay? We haven't even started and I can already tell you guys are uncomfortable. Does someone want to tell me about that?"

Sarah, the young woman who was sexually abused, cries out, "No fucking way. I mean, you expect me to forgive the asshole who abused me for so long? Are you nuts? No way! He made my life hell. And now, as part of my treatment, I am supposed to forgive him for what he did? Absolutely not."

I am in shock. Sarah said exactly what is on my mind. I look around. The other women are nodding.

"I agree," *says Nyla.* "This isn't about them. This is about me. Why should I make them feel better for what they did by forgiving them? They don't deserve to be forgiven. I'm sorry, but that's not fair. They should be here asking *me* for my forgiveness. They should be apologizing to *me*, and you want me to just give my forgiveness away? I can't."

I can't speak. I'm not sure what words will come out of my mouth if I do. I am totally shocked at the reactions of the other women. How is it possible that we all are thinking the same thing? They hardly ever talk unless they are called on. I don't know what to think about what is happening.

"Look, guys, this isn't about excusing anyone from the responsibility of what he or she did. In fact, it's quite the opposite. You can't forgive someone who is innocent of all wrongdoings, right?"

I want to nod in agreement, but I stare at the floor. My stomach starts to hurt. I want to go home.

"Look, this is about you and getting well. Moving on. Being emotionally and physically healthy. It's about taking control of your past. It's about leaving the hurt and the abuse and the neglect behind you and moving forward to something better. This is a huge, scary step. I realize that. But it's a necessary one. How many of you would have the courage, if I were to bring each of your offenders in here, to confront them face-to-face with what they did to you? Could you tell them how badly they'd hurt you? Could you make them understand how devastating what they did to you was? And if you did, would they take responsibility for it? Would they say they were sorry and want to make it up to you?"

Silence.

I start to cry.

"The fact of the matter is that most of those people aren't strong enough individuals to see past their own issues to realize how much what they do affects other people. They will spend their lives continuing to hurt, abuse, and neglect the ones they love. Most of them when confronted with their own behavior wouldn't be strong enough to admit their wrongdoing and apologize for it. So, you need to accept that up front. This isn't about them. It's about you. So what if they won't take ownership of their actions? So what if they won't apologize? Your future happiness does not lie with them. It lies with you. Right here. Tonight. *You* have the keys to opening up some old wounds, dealing with them, and then sealing them up forever. They are *your* emotional scars, but they don't have to be fatal wounds. Don't give them that power! Let's work through this pain, together, and move on. Can we do that? Together?"

Teardrops blot my sweatshirt. My sleeves are wet where I've wiped my nose on them. Someone, I don't know who, hands me a tissue.

Can I go to the bathroom? I need a moment, okay?

All eyes are on me.

I'll only be a moment, okay? I wasn't expecting this; I really wasn't. Or, maybe I should go. It's obvious that I'm upset already. I don't think I can think clearly or do what you want me to do. But now that I know it's coming, maybe I can try it again Thursday.

"Vanessa, you have to push yourself here. Don't hide behind your hurt. Go to the bathroom, take a moment, and then come back. You are a valuable part of this group. We need you."

Need me? For what? I sit here and write what you want to me write and cry. That's it!

"We know."

Okay! So what difference does it make if I'm here or not? I could just as easily cry at home.

"You're right. But when you cry at home, do you know why you're crying or are you just crying?"

What?

"Think about it. Here, you know exactly why you're crying. A memory from your past has surfaced and you've been forced to deal with it once and for all. You think about it, you write about it, we talk about it, and we move on. *You* move on. The things we've talked about have been painful, but once we've gone over them and talked about some things and you start to see some connections, it takes that emotional power away. They're just memories. They can't hurt you the way they have in the past. Right?"

I am shocked. I sit down. I had never thought about it that way before.

"Look, I'll prove it to you. Open your notebook. Find something you wrote about a few weeks ago."

I flip through my notebook and settle on a page.

"Okay. Skim read what you wrote. Go on."

So I do.

"Now. What do you think about what you wrote?"

Well, it's very detailed.

"Okay. And do you remember the event?"

Yes, I wrote about it.

"No, I mean, now, do you remember the event?"

Yes.

"But you aren't crying."

I wasn't.

"You were crying, a lot, when you first wrote about this topic. But now, you are able to look at that entry and remember that event without being so upset. Why is that?"

I don't know.

"Are you sure? Do you have any ideas?"

No.

"You have finally dealt with those feelings. They can't hurt you anymore. All of those memories and feelings came flooding back when you wrote about that event the first time. It was like being there all over again. But now that you've written about it and we've talked about it, your mind sees that event in a different way. The event may be sad, but it isn't devastating."

So now what?

"Put that event, those feelings, away. You can remember them anytime you want to and they won't be crippling. You're at peace with them. Believe it or not, your heart has healed a little."

So what does forgiveness have to do with all of this?

"Each of you has people you need to forgive in order for your spirit to feel that there has been some sort of resolution. There are lots of ways to do this, but the one I want you guys to do is in the form of a letter. Now here's the tricky part. I want each of you to write not one but *two* letters. The first letter needs to be to you, from the person who hurt you the most. The second letter is your response to the first letter. Does that make sense? You are pretending to be the person who hurt you and then you are going to reply to that person with your own letter. Now you can say whatever you want to in these letters, but in your response letter, you must forgive the person who wrote you the first letter. The purpose of these letters is to heal, so be honest. I'm going to ask each of you to read these letters out loud, so be ready for that, okay?"

Can I go to that bathroom now?

"Are you going to secretly sneak out the back door?"

I smile.

No, not anymore.

———————

Dear Vanessa,

It has taken me years to work up the courage to write this letter to you. I don't think you can imagine how painful this is for me to write, because in doing so, I am finally taking responsibility for some of the things I might have said and done to you over the years, and that's hard for me to do. When I think of how many times I must have hurt you, it makes my heart ache. You are one of the greatest things to ever happen in my life, and to think I hurt you so deeply is almost more than I can bear.

It would be foolish for me to ask for your forgiveness, so I won't. But I do hope you will read this letter with an open mind and heart and realize how truly sorry I am for everything that I am about to mention. It was never my intention to make your life miserable, or to make you feel bad about yourself, but I know I did.

I have never done this before, so please be patient. I am going to start at the beginning, because I want you to know that I really am sorry and acknowledge all the things I did to hurt you.

When you were born, it was the happiest day of my life. When I looked at you for the first time, I instantly fell in love with you. I thought you were the most beautiful thing I had ever seen. I had such big hopes for your future and secretly promised to make your happiness my only goal in life. But then something changed. I can't put my finger on it, so I don't know whether the change happened over time or overnight, but one day I realized I didn't look at you the same way. Maybe I was naive, but I didn't realize how much time you and your brothers would take up in my life, and I started to resent you for it. I had my own goals and dreams, and you interfered with them. I'm not saying this was your fault; it's just a fact.

You had such a strong personality, and you made me feel like a bad parent sometimes. I could tell you were mad at me or didn't agree with me on something and it broke my heart. You didn't always do what I wanted you to do, and that made me mad. I called you names and hit you to try to make you behave. I wanted you to be obedient, and you were some of the time, but not all of the time. It was unrealistic of me to expect that of you, but I did, just like my father expected it of me. I tried to break your will because we were going head-to-head against each other most of the time, and I couldn't have it! So, I said more hateful things and hit you even harder to try to force you to bend to my will. I had to make you understand that you weren't in charge, that *I* was the parent. But you had such a strong will. It's like you came into this world with a plan, and I didn't know how to handle that. I'm sorry.

It's hard for me to write this letter, because I know that my worst fear has come true. I didn't want you to feel as inadequate as a child as I did, but you have, and I am the reason for it. I hated my parents for some of the things they did and said, and I vowed to be a better parent than that. I wasn't. All of my insecurities about myself are tied up in the names I called you. All of the things I feared others were saying about me, I said to you. I could see myself doing that, but I couldn't stop. And you just soaked it all in. I couldn't take it back. If I had apologized to you, it would have made me look weak, and I thought that was worse than being an asshole, so I didn't. I should have.

I wanted to be a good parent, but life got in the way. I believed that if I had enough education, enough life experiences, that I would turn out to be a better man than my father was. I hate to say that wasn't the case.

I'm sorry that I hurt you, Vanessa. I'm sorry that I said things to you that made you hate who you are and question the woman you are becoming. And I hope you will do something I was never able to do: move forward. Move past your hang-ups and insecurities. Believe in yourself. Love yourself enough to take care of yourself, and allow other people to take care of you. I never did because I thought I could do it all on my own. Well, I was wrong, and I have lived a life without the love of others for a long, long time.

I love you and hope you and I will be able to talk about this openly one day in the future.

Love,

Dad

I can't stop shaking. Everything I have ever wanted my dad to say to me has come out through my pen. I can't believe how easy it was for me to pretend to be him. I thought for sure we had nothing in common. Part of me wonders how accurate I am. If he were to read this, would he tear it up and tell me it's bullshit? Would he ever acknowledge that he did something wrong? Part of me doubts it, but for the first time in my life, it doesn't seem to matter. The words I needed to hear are here, in my hands, and I can read them. Absorb them. Accept them. Who cares if I was the one who wrote them? The words are the same. The intention is the same. The meaning is the same. I feel my chest start to relax. Maybe I can do this after all.

Dear Dad,

I cannot tell you how angry I am at you for all the things you have said and done to me over the years. You were the first man I ever laid eyes on. Out of all the men on earth, *you* were the one God entrusted me to. The one He decided was more qualified than any other man on earth to be my father. To protect me. To love me. To show me the skills I would need to navigate through life.

But you failed.

Instead of building me up, you tore me down. You filled my heart with lies, and because they came from you, I believed them. But no more.

My body is a patchwork of scars that physically represent the mental hurts I suffered. I carry within me an insatiable quest for perfection. As part of that tendency, I have struggled with an eating disorder for most of my teen and adult life. You are part of the reason this exists. Did you not realize how damaging your unrealistic expectations were to my self-esteem and body image? Without the pressure you put on me to be, do, and act a certain way as a child, I might have had a more realistic view of myself and my capabilities as an adult. I would have taken pride in the things I can do and not sweated over those I can't. You made me feel like I couldn't do *anything* well.

I have nearly died from the messages you planted in my head. "You're not good enough, Vanessa." "You're selfish, Vanessa." "You would let the goddamned house burn down before you did anything about it." "You delight in the misfortune of others." "You are so stupid, even the Special Olympics wouldn't want you." "You're worthless. I can't stand to have you in my sight."

These words were more powerful than you could have ever imagined, and when I think of them, I think of you. You, the man who was supposed to love me more than anyone else. You, who were supposed to be my greatest source of encouragement. It's a shame you weren't able to fulfill those obligations to me.

I have never had anyone in my life make me feel so small and insignificant. To say that I have hated you for most of my life would be an understatement. Hate doesn't seem to be a strong enough word. I have envisioned your death more times than I can count—you being run over by a dump truck, you being impaled, you being shot, you being killed by a drunk driver. Anything to take you from me. Anything to make the feelings of inadequacy and worthlessness stop.

Part of me wants to forgive you; but the other part of me wants to make your life as painful as mine has been. But I can't. There is no way you will ever know how much I have struggled because of you. But you probably don't care. You have your career and your life back. I am no longer someone who monopolizes your time, and I'm sure that makes you happy.

You are part of the reason I am the way that I am. I learned many behaviors and coping mechanisms from you that have almost cost me my life. But unlike you, I want to move past them. I want to find new ways of expressing myself and better ways to cope with life. The negative messages, the cutting, and the starving myself, they have to stop. *You* have to stop.

You said you couldn't ask me to forgive you, but I do. Not because I want to or because you deserve it, but because *I* do. My mental and emotional health is worth more than the pain I feel by carrying around all of my frustration and anger toward you.

So, it's done. I will never treat someone the way you treated me. I will never make someone feel as bad about themselves as you made me feel, and I will *never* abandon someone I love for my own self-benefit. You are the product of your past, as am I. But *I* refuse to be a prisoner of it. I forgive you, I forgive you, I forgive you.

Your daughter,
Vanessa

I am completely overwhelmed. I never, in a million years, thought I would be able to say the things that I have written. But there they are. I reread what I wrote. This is my chance. My chance to say everything I ever wanted to say to my dad. Did I say everything? Is it clear? Would he even "get it" if he were here to read it himself?

I close my notebook and shut my eyes.

Focus on breathing.

In and out.

In and out.

"Vanessa, are you okay?"

Yeah. It's done.

"How does it feel?"

Like I've run a marathon.

"Did it hurt?"

Like a bitch, but it's done.

"Do you feel empowered?"

Yeah.

"Let me know when you're ready to go over them."

I'm ready now.

"You don't want to take a moment to think about what you wrote?"

No. I don't know how to explain it, but it was like my hand had a mind of its own. So, whatever is on these pages comes directly from my heart. I don't want to mess with it.

"That's fine. Why don't you read your first letter to us."

Dear Vanessa . . .

It's amazing how my memories are stored. Most of my memories are like a strobe light—flicker, fade, focus, quick image, flicker, fade, focus, another image—it's like I can never get a really good look at what I'm trying to remember. Somehow, my brain didn't process the event or feeling deep enough, and so these flickers, these random images, are all that remain.

But then there are others that are so complete, so rich in detail, that I can recall smells, fragments of conversations, patterns on fabrics, faces of those around me. No longer a pulsating strobe light, these memories are a patchwork of sensations, permanently imprinted on my psyche.

What bothers me the most is that I don't feel like I have any control over how my memories are stored. Things that I vowed I would remember forever have, with time, faded into oblivion. Names, faces, and events have melded into one image, losing all relevance of time or circumstance. I try to imagine the boy I went to the prom with, and I can't. I have to pull out an old picture album to jog my memory. I try to remember details of my wedding that I swore I would remember for as long as I lived. I can't. A wedding video and a scattering of pictures are all that remain of one of the best days of my life. But ask me to remember what the boy said to me on the bus in the sixth grade, and I can tell you every word, every look, every hand gesture he made.

I hate it.

I hate that of the two parents, my mother was my favorite, yet few details of my early interactions with her remain in my memory. We read out loud together for hours at a time, yet I can't tell you what books we read. But ask me what book my father read to me out loud over the course of several weeks, and I can tell you it was The Lord of the Rings. *I know my mother did lots of things to surprise me, but I can't quite put my fingers on any one specific example. But ask me what my father brought me home from a business trip or something, and I could tell you instantly.*

I hate my father, yet there are more details about him in my mind than there are of my mother.

I hate it.

I feel guilty about it.

I resent it.

How could I possibly have allowed myself to absorb so many memories of my father when I felt so much anger toward him? Why didn't I shut myself off to him emotionally and instead just soak up all the good thoughts and deeds my mother tried to plant in my mind?

How could I have allowed someone so hateful to make me hate myself?

I look at my arms.

My legs.

My eyes.

I don't recognize the person standing there.

When did I become so old? So road weary? So fearful?

I look away.

The scissors have been lying on the counter for a while now.

They are new, and they speak to me.

I close my eyes and clench my teeth. I have to fight this. I can't do this anymore; I promised.

From the far recesses of my mind a voice, my voice, cries out:

The reason you absorbed all the negative messages and experiences of your past is because they were true.

No, they're not!

Yes, they are. Do you think your mother would have allowed your father to speak that way to you if it weren't true?

You lie! She couldn't say anything; he would have turned on her!

A mother will tell you the truth. Her not correcting your father means what he said was true. You are a disappointment. You are selfish. You are only in this place because of your refusal to believe what you know down deep inside yourself is true.

I pick up the scissors. I open the blades and bring them closer to my eyes. I want to see the serrated edges and the cut of the blade. I want to know the thing that will take me away from this place. My salvation. My repentance.

You are a bad person, Vanessa. That's why you hurt so much. A good person with a good heart wouldn't hurt nearly as much as you do. You have to do this. Be sorry. Be remorseful. Show the world how sorry you are.

I look at my eyes again in the mirror, trying to find some reprieve, but there is none.

The first cut is small. Purposeful. Deep.

I cut on a spot that I've cut before, so it doesn't bleed right away. The scar tissue protects the skin beneath it and I fight to rip the top layers of skin away.

My cuts are precise and neat. I know they will scar and I want them to look "nice."

The scissors are in my left hand, poised on my right wrist. White. Flawless. An empty canvas to house my pain.

Using the tips of the scissors, I cut a small triangle into the flesh.

Snip.

Snip.

Snip.

Three small cuts. One triangle of flesh clinging to the blades.

I put it into my mouth and roll it over my tongue.

It is salty and rubbery between my teeth.

I stick my tongue out and see it there on my tongue . . . a tangible
part of who Vanessa is, and I swallow.

I grab a piece of toilet paper and start on the second triangle.

Snip.

Snip.

Snip.

And a third.

I cannot wipe the blood away fast enough to see what I'm doing.

Triangles number four, five, and six are done by instinct.

I'm sorry! I'm sorry! I'm sorry!

Go ahead, Vanessa. How sorry are you?

My eyes blur. Tears have started to hit my arm.

I'm sorry I disappointed you!

I'm sorry I wasn't the child you wanted me to be!

I'm sorry for being such a bad person!

I . . .

Knock. Knock. Knock.

"Vanessa? My love? What are doing in there? Are you okay? Why
are you crying?"

I stop. Catch a glimpse of myself in the mirror. I look like a were-
wolf interrupted from devouring its prey. Lips snarled, eyes squinted,
face red and sweaty.

"Vanessa? Why is the door locked?"

Breathe.

Wait.

Maybe he'll go away.

"Vanessa? Open this door. What are you doing? Come on, open
the door!"

It's okay. I'm going to take a shower.

I pause, hysterical with fear that he will try to open the door, but
it's locked, and he doesn't force the issue.

A moment of silence. I pray he has left me alone.

I frantically try to turn the water on in the sink as quietly as I can.
I stick the scissors under the stream.

Another knock.

My heart stops. I have one foot in the bathtub, one out. My arm is dripping blood down its porcelain sides.

"Vanessa? It's not even four o'clock in the afternoon. What are you doing?"

Desperate for a rational excuse for what I'm doing, I flush the toilet to cover up any sounds.

Just a minute . . .

My eyes fall on the alcohol and cotton balls still on the countertop. Dripping blood and water onto the floor, I scramble to put things away. Cover my arm. Wipe my eyes.

Hang on. I'm almost out!

I step back into the shower and use a sponge to try to wash the blood drops away. I check the curtain for telltale signs.

Safe.

My husband, trusting my every word, doesn't knock again. If he suspects anything, he says nothing.

Crying, I let the water hit my arm. It stings. It's pink. White where the blades have crisscrossed my wrist. The triangles white and jagged.

It starts as a whisper.

Vanessa . . .

You can't hide from me, you know. We're not through. The ritual is not complete.

I look at the disposable razor lying on the side of the tub.

Finish this. Do what you have to do.

I pick up the razor and look at it. At my arm. At my chest and legs getting wet in the shower spray.

If I drag it, just so . . . even up the edges a little bit.

Three red lines appear on my forearm.

Go on.

Once more. Deeper this time. The skin flays under the blade.

Three more red lines appear on my forearm. Six parallel lines of remorse spilling red onto the porcelain tub.

I close my eyes and run my arm through the water.

Red appears. Put it in the water. Red disappears.

Eventually, the red stops appearing.

The triangles are holes . . . white and swollen in a sea of pink stripes.

I sit down in the tub and rest my face on my knees.

I put my neck under the spray and let it fall into my ears.

Deafening.

Like being in a waterfall.

I hate what I've done.

I hate the lies I've got to create to cover it up.

I hate the scars these cuts will create.

And I hate that I will have to go back to the group and share with them my relapse.

I guess forgiving someone else really is easier than forgiving myself.

"**So what made you do that?** Did you have a bad day? Did some-one say something that triggered something in you?"

I was afraid.

"Afraid of what?"

Of not knowing who I am.

"What do you mean?"

We've been doing so much work on confronting our past and dealing with the pain there—forgiving other people, looking ahead to a happier and healthier future—that I guess I was scared.

"Scared about what?"

Scared because I know what I need and want and I may never get it. Maybe I don't deserve it. And that thought makes me feel like I am an idiot for even wanting something from my father in the first place. How many times will I shed tears over that man? He's not worth it.

I know the letters we wrote in group aren't real. But it felt so good to read the words I wrote and imagine my father saying them to me. But I know my father would *never* say those things and it makes me sad. A part of me longs for him to be honest with me—to validate the feelings I've felt for so long, to take some responsibility for his part of the shaping of who I am. I know that will never happen.

"But if you know that up front, why is that so hurtful? You can't expect someone to give you what they don't have. Your father doesn't have what you need. You are looking for reassurance from someone who can't give it to you. Maybe he doesn't give it to you out of spite, or perhaps he just doesn't know how. The bottom line is that your father was not and is not the person you need him to be. But you have to accept him as he is. He isn't going to change. Only *you* can change the way you respond to him and the messages he gave you."

I don't want to hear that. My father is a smart man. How can he not know what I need to hear? It seems so obvious.

"Vanessa. In group sessions, we talked about how our feelings of anger and resentment hurt only us. Look at yourself. Do you think your father knows how badly he has hurt you? Do you think he has any possible way of knowing the negative impact his words have had on your sense of self? The answer is unequivocally no. Even if your father were here for you to talk to, there is no way you could *ever* describe the amount of pain he has caused you. If you are looking for absolution or acceptance from your father, then I'm afraid you are setting yourself up for failure. You and I need to work on getting you to a place of self-acceptance and love that is freestanding from the opinions of other people. What you need to realize is that Vanessa is a good person because you are. Period. Having your father agree or disagree doesn't change the way things are, only your perception of them. Does that make sense?"

On the one hand, I agree with you. But on the other hand, I feel like I have to keep trying. Maybe one day he will be in a place where he can tell me what I need to hear.

"Are you willing to spend the rest of your life waiting on something that may or may not happen?"

I don't know. I don't want to. I want to get to a place where it doesn't matter anymore. I mean, what if he died and we never had a chance to talk to each other again. Part of me thinks that would be better because then I would know 100 percent that I would never get from him what I'm looking for. As long as he is out there somewhere, there is a chance.

"So let's talk best-case scenario for a moment. Your father appears, he hears what you need from him, and he tells you he's sorry. He sits down with you, holds your hands, traces your scars with his fingertips, looks into your eyes, and tells you everything you want him to say. Then what? Is your life on a new course? Are you fixed? Is the need to cut totally gone?"

I've thought about that, too. And as much as I'd love for that to happen, it scares me even more than never talking to my father again.

"Why is that? You'd be getting what you've wanted for so long!"

I don't know what Vanessa is going to be like once all of these bad parts of me are fixed. I'm so used to hurting that I can't imagine a life without it. It's a part of me. If you take all those familiar parts away, what's left? I feel like part of who I am involves hurting myself. If I come to terms with my reasons for cutting, then who have I become? If I have a reconciliation with my father one day, a big part of my spirit won't have a hole in it. That will mean I've become a new person. That scares me.

"So that's why you cut yourself?"

You know the feeling you get on a roller coaster? As you crest over the first hill, you get the excited this-is-going-to-be-great-I'm-going-to-throw-up-what-was-I-thinking feeling in the pit of your stomach. That was me after I left group. I'm so afraid of asking for what I want, but equally afraid of what will happen if I do. I don't know what to wish for. Do I wish for something and then deal with the disappointment when I don't get it? Am I strong enough to handle more rejection? Do I feel bad for wishing for something in the first place because I doubt my worthiness? Or, do I just resign myself to the fact that no matter how hard I wish, what I want is impossible, so it will never happen? The feelings were too much. I looked at myself in the mirror and asked what Vanessa wanted. There wasn't an answer. I stood there for what seemed like an hour and a million thoughts were running through my head. I hadn't planned on cutting, I really hadn't. But the longer I tried to sort out my feelings, the more feelings erupted to the surface. It's like I went from being in a totally rational and controlled place to one of absolute chaos. I thought about the things I'd written in my letters and I started to feel bad about how honest I'd been. I felt desperate. I started to wonder what the other women in the group thought of me. I started to wonder what you thought of me. And before I knew it, the voices started again. But I felt strong. I felt empowered. I looked myself in the eyes and told myself I was *not* going to be weak. I was *not* going to resort to cutting to feel in control. I told myself I was better.

And you know what? I *lost!* I'm really trying to be honest with myself and make some changes, and for what? For this?

I thrust my wrist out for her to see it.

For new scars? For new lies? For new proof that I need more help than I might ever be able to get?

"Vanessa, I think you're wrong. I think you are getting better. Are you cured as you said? No. Does that mean you'll never be? Probably not. But it's too early. You are in a really emotional place right now."

So now what?

"You have to keep going. Keep plodding ahead. Keep going into emotional places you don't want to go, so that we can free you from the power that lies there."

But I want to stop cutting! I don't want to be ninety years old in the old folk's home and trying to explain what I'm doing to myself!

"Okay. Then trust me. Things may get worse before they get better, and that's normal. You are being forced to change your thinking a little bit and to confront some things from your past. You're right, you *don't* want to be doing this forever. So do it now. You've already come this far; keep going."

You haven't asked me about the voices.

"Well, what do you want me to know about them?"

They were different this time.

"How so?"

Usually most of the voices are authoritative and clearly in my dad's tone of voice. But this time they were different. The voices were *all* mine.

"**Last week we talked** about forgiving other people. Tonight, we are going to talk about forgiving yourself. Before you can forgive another person, you must forgive yourself. Everyone makes mistakes and feels regret at some point in his or her life. Usually, mistakes are places of growth and knowledge. A person gleans what he or she can from the experience and moves on. But this is something each of you finds difficult to do. You harbor guilt and responsibility and insulate yourself as a way of punishing yourself for not being perfect. Now, as important as last week was to the healing process, tonight's session is even more critical, because tonight each of you is going to have to talk about and accept the fact that you are not now, nor will you ever be, perfect. You will never be able to make everyone else happy. And no matter how hard you try, you will never be able to take back, change, or undo any of the hurts that were done to you. Tonight, we are going to go around the room and make forgiveness statements to each other. Each of you longs to hear that you are forgiven for something but believes you don't deserve it. Tonight, we are going to practice forgiving each other as a model for how we can forgive ourselves. Now, before we can do that, we have to identify what it is that each of you feels you need to be forgiven for. So that's what I want you to write about first. I need you to make a list of things, situations, and so forth that you feel bad about and want to be forgiven for. Once your list is complete, we are going to exchange lists with each other. You are going to pick one thing off your list that you most wish to be forgiven for. You are going to tell us about that situation and then someone in the group is going to forgive you. I want you to focus on the words being said here tonight. Understand that when someone says she forgives you, she does and your trespass is forgotten. You don't have to do anything else to earn her forgiveness. You acknowledge what you did, express remorse, you are forgiven, and that's that. The first step is to write down all the things you think you need to be forgiven for. It can be anything you want—large, small, anything."

Wow. Didn't see this coming. No clue what to write.

I start to chew on the end of my pen.

I stare at the floor.

Forgiveness . . . anything . . .

Vanessa's Forgiveness List:

1. Stealing a small, red plastic bear from kindergarten classroom because it fit in my pocket

2. Getting younger brothers into trouble on purpose

3. Calling younger brothers names, and when they cried, trying to buy them off with pennies out of my piggy bank

4. Refusing to apologize to my mother when I made her cry

5. Cheating on a seventh-grade history quiz

6. Forging my parents' signatures on progress reports for an entire semester before I got caught

7. Flirting with a boy whom I knew liked me and convincing him to ask me to the prom to get revenge on my ex-boyfriend, and then dumping him the day after prom

8. Lying to my parents

9. Disobeying my parents while on a sleepover and destroying a friendship in the process

10. Telling my mother I hated her when she was only trying to save my life

11. Not meeting other people's expectations

12. Being jealous of other people who are better than me

13. Being too scared of rejection to be really open and honest with other people

14. Calling unnecessary attention to myself

15. Pretending to be sick for three days just so I could stay home and watch *The Brady Bunch in the Grand Canyon* on television

16. Not taking care of the body God has given me

"Now our second step is for you to prioritize your list. What are the top five or six things you want to be forgiven for? The top things that you feel are a burden to your soul? These are the things we want to address. So, I need you to take a look at your list and put a star by the ones that you feel are the most pressing for you."

Vanessa's Forgiveness List:

1. Stealing a small, red plastic bear from kindergarten classroom because it fit in my pocket

2. Getting younger brothers into trouble on purpose

3. Calling younger brothers names, and when they cried, trying to buy them off with pennies out of my piggy bank

*4. Refusing to apologize to my mother when I made her cry

5. Cheating on a seventh-grade history quiz

6. Forging my parents' signatures on progress reports for an entire semester before I got caught

*7. Flirting with a boy whom I knew liked me and convincing him to ask me to the prom to get revenge on my ex-boyfriend, and then dumping him the day after prom

8. Lying to my parents

9. Disobeying my parents while on a sleepover and destroying a friendship in the process

. 10. Telling my mother I hated her when she was only trying to save my life

*11. Not meeting other people's expectations

*12. Being jealous of other people who are better than me

*13. Being too scared of rejection to be really open and honest with other people

14. Calling unnecessary attention to myself

15. Pretending to be sick for three days just so I could stay home and watch *The Brady Bunch in the Grand Canyon* on television

*16. Not taking care of the body God has given me

"All right, now look at the things you have a star by. These are the things we want to talk about tonight. We are going to pass our lists around so that everyone can read them. Then we are going to fold them up, shuffle them, and hand them back out. The idea is that the list you end up with should not be your own list. Once you get the new list, you are going to call on that person and go over the things on her list. Let that person tell you about the things she starred, and then you are going to say, I forgive you for . . . Okay? No matter what that person says, you tell her, I forgive you for . . . . There is something incredibly powerful in the whole confession and forgiveness cycle. Are we ready? Any questions before we begin? Okay, pass your lists around."

There are so many secrets in my heart. Some I put on my list and many I did not. For as much as I want to trust my group mates, I can't. I'm not even sure I can trust myself. So I keep those inside for a while and start off with things that, in the whole scheme of things, aren't really that important.

But not everyone feels the same way I do.

I am shocked by some of the things that are written on the lists.

And then I am ashamed that I am shocked. At least they had the courage to do this all the way.

In the end, I pull Nyla's list. She is a kindergarten teacher in her thirties with an eating disorder.

Apparently, as she was leaving school one day, one of her students didn't use the crosswalk and darted across traffic. It was pouring down rain, and the kids were in a hurry to get home. She never saw the kid and accidentally ran him over. The child lived, but this close call of nearly killing one of her own students was almost more than she could bear.

I barely start my forgiveness statement before she starts crying hysterically.

"I never saw him! I mean, it was pouring down rain, and the kids know . . . the kids know they are supposed to use the crosswalks! We go over it all the time. Why would he do that? Why wasn't I paying more attention? Why didn't I swerve? He could have died! I could have killed him! He was in the hospital because of me. Do you know how awful that is? To go to school the next day and have to explain to the school board that there was an accident? How can his family ever feel good about sending him to my school again? He's not safe there!"

I am speechless.

Her sobs continue.

I don't know what to say. I want to ask if the parents sued, but I don't. It seems rude.

Nyla. I forgive you for running over that student. It was an accident; you didn't do it on purpose.

"No, I didn't, but you can't imagine how awful this was . . . pouring down rain . . . police reports, ambulances . . . phone calls to the parents."

I look at my therapist, and she nods. So I say it again.

Nyla. I forgive you for running over that student. It was an accident; you didn't do it on purpose.

"How can I forgive myself for my carelessness? I should have been paying more attention. I should have seen him running across the road. But he didn't even have an umbrella or a bright coat. Just him. Soaking wet. Screaming!"

Nyla. I forgive you for running over that student. It was an accident; you didn't do it on purpose.

I start again.

Nyla. It's done. The kid is okay and you are okay, too. Forgive yourself. Let it go. You aren't going to convince me *not* to forgive you, so accept it. I don't think you're a horrible person. It was an accident. I forgive you.

We all start to cry.

In reality, this kid's parents were the only ones who could forgive Nyla for what she had done. But the chances were, she would never hear that from them. To hear those words now, the words she had longed to hear for so long, was truly overwhelming.

"I'm so sorry. I'm so sorry. I just didn't see him. I'm so sorry."

Nyla, you are forgiven.

A sniff. And then a quiet "thank you."

I don't want a turn. I don't want to be as vulnerable as Nyla has been, so I allow everyone else in the group to go before me. I figure if they take long enough, time will run out, group will be dismissed, and I will be off the hook.

No such luck.

"Ladies, I know it's late, but would you mind staying a little longer? I don't want anyone to leave here tonight without having a chance to feel some sort of absolution for the things on her list. Vanessa has been really patient and I want to give her a chance before we leave for the evening. Is that okay with everyone?"

I pray for someone to say, "No, I have a long commute." Or, "Can we do this next time? I really do have other plans."

But one look into everyone's eyes and I know I am stuck for the long haul.

Great. Fan-freaking-tastic.

Sarah has my list.

"Vanessa, I forgive you for not apologizing to your mother when you made her cry."

I stare straight ahead.

No response.

She looks at me.

"Aren't you going to say anything?"

I just sit there.

Do you want to know why I never apologized to my mother? Even after I made her cry?

I look down at my shirt and start to play with a stray string I find there.

I couldn't. It didn't matter how much I wanted to say it, I couldn't.

In my house you were told to say you were sorry, even if you didn't feel like it. And then when you did say it, it was like you weren't believed, like you weren't really sorry. So I just quit saying it.

When I'd get into trouble, I'd be told, "Now tell your brothers you're sorry." And couldn't. I would be too mad or upset to feel true remorse, and so I would stand there. It meant I'd get into more trouble, but I didn't care. I didn't want to say something I didn't feel. And that would make my mom or dad even angrier. So at the beginning, I did. I would say I was sorry and then I'd get into trouble for not sounding sincere. So I quit saying it.

"Go to your room and you stay there until you can come out and apologize!"

Nine times out of ten, I wouldn't come out. Dinner would pass by and I would fall asleep feeling even worse than I had at the beginning because no one seemed to understand why I couldn't say what they wanted me to say. I believed I was a bad person because I couldn't put my feelings aside and just say something as easy as "I'm sorry" when others wanted me to.

Years passed and I wouldn't say, "I'm sorry." It became this running joke and eventually turned into this whole idea that because I wouldn't say I was sorry, I was self-centered and totally uncaring—like I didn't care for other people's feelings.

But it wasn't true! Eventually I was sorry, but usually not for the things my parents would think. If I had said what I really felt, and said what I was *really* sorry for, it would have made things worse. I knew it, and so I chose to remain silent.

It sounds so trivial now, but I still believe this way. I only apologize when I am really sure, in my heart, of what I am sorry for. Then, and only then do I say anything.

How many people say they're sorry all the time without really being sorry? Their apology is worthless, empty. I didn't want to be like that. So I didn't say it, and when I was ready to say it, it was too late. People had already made up their minds about me, and it wasn't true.

I start to cry.

I used to spend hours in my room making a written apology. I would decorate it or write a poem on it, and I would sneak out of my room, listen for distant voices, and then go into my parents' bedroom and prop it up on their pillows. These notes weren't acknowledged, so I don't even know if they read them. But they were sincere and from the heart. Much more so than if I had said it halfheartedly hours before.

But it didn't matter. I was told I was selfish and unfeeling and someone who cared only for myself.

I have spent my entire life proving that isn't true.

What's funny, though, what's freakin' hysterical is that my parents didn't say they were sorry *for anything!*

It was understood that they were the parents and so there was supposed to be a good reason for whatever they did, right or not. If you questioned them or wanted to know why, you were told, "Look, I'm the parent here, not you. I don't have to explain myself to you. Do what I'm telling you to do!"

So you quit asking, and you believe in your childlike heart that your parents are perfect, that they never make any mistakes, because if they did, they would say they were sorry, too. But they never do.

Do you know how bad it makes you feel when *you* are the only one who feels like a complete screwup? I mean, it was like everyone else in my house was perfect, and then there was me. A complete disappointment and someone who was so selfish, according to my father, that "she would let the house burn down!"

The more I was told that, the more I believed in my heart that if the house were ever to *really* catch on fire, I just might let it.

I feel like someone is moving my mouth. I want to quit talking, but the words keep coming. I desperately try to make eye contact with someone in the group in an effort to beg someone to shut me up, but no one is looking at me. I've made them uncomfortable and they are looking everywhere but at me.

I think that's why I loved stuffed animals so much and reading. I could escape my life. I could be a person who wasn't a failure, who didn't fall short of other people's expectations, and who wasn't judged for being something I couldn't be: just like everyone else.

Even now, as an adult, I won't say I'm sorry until I really am. I see other people say it in the heat of the moment just to smooth things over, and you know it's not true. So why do it? Why patronize someone just so you don't have to be mad anymore?

So I don't.

It has taken my husband a long time to figure this one out, but he finally understands. And when I say it, it is sincere, it is remorseful, and it is *real*.

I sniff and someone passes me a tissue.

Finally. A life buoy in a sea of sadness.

I take it without looking at who has passed it to me.

I'm sorry.

I feel about three feet tall.

How I wish the earth would open up and swallow me whole!

"For what?"

For this.

I look around now, face flushed, palms sweaty.

For believing that my feelings were more important than someone else's immediate reassurance that I hadn't hurt them on purpose.

I know that by *not* telling them I was sorry, right away, it meant that I did hurt them on purpose, and *that* is what I am really sorry for.

But I'm *not* selfish, I'm *not* someone who delights in the misfortune of others!

"I know. But you don't seem to be convinced."

I can't believe my therapist has the audacity to say this to me!

I am! Why is it that when I said I was sorry, no one thought it was sincere?

I find my therapist's eyes across the room and stare into them. Darts shoot from my eyes into her attitude of disbelief. What will it take for her to know how sincere I am?

I pull up my sleeves.

You want to see how sorry I am? I'll show you!

THIS! THIS IS HOW SORRY I AM!

The cuts and triangles I made earlier in the week have grown red and angry. I refuse to give them a chance to heal. I have pulled scabs from the holes multiple times. And in an effort to punish myself further, I have denied myself bandages or antiseptic ointment.

I don't have to tell you I'm sorry. *This* is my "I'm sorry!" It's my apology to the world for *everything!* For being born! For being a disappointment! For wanting to fly with eagles when I live with chickens! For wanting to be more than I was told I could be.

I pull my sleeve back down violently. I inadvertently bang my wrist on the arm of the chair and a searing flash of pain runs up my arm and down into my fingers. Secretly, I hope I've made the wounds bleed again.

A small voice permeates my consciousness.

"Vanessa."

I reach for another tissue.

"Vanessa, look at me."

"We forgive you. For all of it. Everything. We believe you, and we forgive you."

Self-righteous witch.

I feel like everyone is staring at me. Disgusted.

I feel dirty and ashamed.

I've never shown the others what I mean by self-injury. Hearing about it and seeing it are two different things. Now they've seen what I can do and have all the information they need to judge me for it.

Can I go now? I want to go home.

"Yes, but first I want to make sure you are okay. Do you feel better? Do you feel like you took a step forward tonight?"

Is she kidding me? What step forward? That I have officially cleared up any confusion about whether or not I'm a crazy person?

What step are you talking about?

"It's one thing to engage in a behavior and it's another to take ownership of it. You did that tonight. For the first time ever, you took complete ownership of what you do to yourself and you shared it with others. Isn't that liberating?"

Liberating? No. It's not liberating. It's scary as hell. I can only imagine what people in here think of me now. I'm not sure I even want to know. Is this what group is all about?

"No. Group is giving you a chance to revisit some critical events of your past in an effort to see how they fit into your present behaviors and addictions. Tonight, we worked on forgiveness and coming to terms with the reality that you haven't done anything so horrible you can't be forgiven for it. You deserve to be forgiven, Vanessa."

Okay. Fine. So tonight I took a step. But I'm ready to stop taking steps. It's too hard, and I'm tired.

"But you have to keep going, Vanessa. You have to believe that what you're doing here is creating a new emotional life for yourself. And that's what you want, right?"

I nod.

"Well then. I guess I'll be seeing you again on Tuesday at six o'clock."

Great. Another chance to make a complete ass of myself.

I was in middle school when my peers decided I was a social outcast, unworthy of their time and attention. I was made fun of.

Mercilessly.

It didn't matter what I wore or what I did. I was the subject of passing notes, dirty names, and complete ridicule.

Naturally curly hair, braces and neck gear, glasses, and non–name brand clothes. You add to that my intellectual leanings, and it was a formula for popularity disaster.

If I went into the lunchroom and found an empty seat, I would sit there.

Invariably, not two minutes later, someone would come by, usually with a group of other "beautiful people," and say, "Hey, you're in my seat. I sit there. I just went to get some milk and now you're in my seat."

Being the social retard that I was, I would scoop up my lunch and leave.

I never had the courage or self-confidence to tell them to go screw themselves. And so I would leave, and I would be the one who felt totally screwed.

Before too long, I quit going to lunch. I would ask one of my teachers if I could come in and study or help them and eat my lunch alone.

In PE, I was the one who was made to cry. I would wait until everyone else had gone into the showers to change, and then I would jump in, hose off, and then scramble to collect my clothes before they were tossed all over the locker room. Sometimes I made it. Sometimes I didn't. More than once I was late to class because I'd spent half an hour trying to get my shorts, socks, and bra off the top of the locker bins.

"Hey, Vanessa. You're a carpenter's dream! You're flat as a board!"

"Hey, Vanessa. Do you have to stick your finger into a socket to get your hair to look like that?"

"Hey, Vanessa. What's it like to not have any friends?"

And on and on it would go.

Day in and day out.

I cried after school every day.

My mother's advice was worthless: "Don't let them know they hurt you. If you ignore them, they will stop. They only bother you because they know it upsets you. Ignore them, and they'll stop."

So I did.

But they didn't stop.

They stepped it up a notch.

"Vanessa, why don't you come and sit with us at lunch? We're sorry for saying mean things."

Like a dumb ass, I would say, "Really?"

I wanted to believe them so much.

So I would go.

"Why don't you go find us some seats and we'll meet you once we get out of the lunch line."

I didn't know that these kids had already told all their friends about the setup, and that there wouldn't be any seat for me.

I walked around and found several together.

"Hey, you can't sit there. This seat is saved."

Sorry. And I'd scoop up my things and move.

I'd hear them laughing hysterically as I walked away.

Try again.

"Hey, you can't sit there. This seat is saved."

Sorry.

More laughter.

I looked back at the first place I'd tried to sit and realized that seat was still empty.

There wasn't anyone to sit there; they just didn't want me to sit there.

I never did find my so-called friends and ended up throwing my lunch away.

"Hey, Vanessa, we're sorry you didn't find us. It was for the best anyway. There weren't enough seats for everyone to sit together, so we had to split up."

Yeah, right.

In the months to come, they would invite me to lunch with them again.

And like an idiot, I would go.

I didn't want to.

But I did.

I wanted their approval so much. And so even though I knew it would be a disaster, I went.

"Are you going to Brenda's party?"

I didn't even know she was having a party.

"We're all going. It's going to be great. A sleepover. Movies. Sneaking out to toilet paper houses. Why don't you come?"

I wasn't invited.

"I don't think she'd care. Come!"

Later on that day Brenda approached me.

"I'm sorry I didn't invite you to the party. My mom said I could only invite my dearest friends, and so I did. No hard feelings, right?"

No, of course not, you stuck-up little bitch.

No, of course not.

"Oh, good."

I have been to only a handful of sleepovers in my life. I am not a night owl, and so I usually fall asleep before midnight anyway.

The biggest part of a sleepover was deciding whose sleeping bag was next to whose.

"Hey, Vanessa. Can you move your bag? I want to sleep next to Mary."

So I did.

"Hey, Vanessa. Can I move you over here? I want to sleep next to Stacy."

So they did.

Before the night was over, I would be spooning the hearth.

I hated going to sleepovers because I was never really wanted. I was the token nice girl who would entertain the mother while the other girls went off and played Truth or Dare or Light as a Feather, Stiff as a Board.

And so I quit asking to go.

Eventually, I just wasn't asked to go at all.

And so into my shell I crawled.

I was the outcast.

Teacher's pet.

The nerd who everyone sucked up to for help, but no one wanted to be friends with.

"Shhh! Here she comes. Hey, Vanessa. What's it like being a virgin? I don't remember."

Who says I'm a virgin?

"Well, you are, aren't you?"

I'd rather not say.

"Oh, come on! You either are or you're not."

And then their eyes lit up.

"Maybe this nerd act of yours is just that. Maybe you really have had sex and just haven't said anything!"

Later that afternoon word got out that I wasn't a virgin.

So, of course, to defend my honor, I yelled that I was.

My entire history class had a field day with that one.

"V. V. Nice! Vanessa is a virgin, Vanessa is a virgin!"

I wanted to die.

I didn't understand why these kids didn't pick on someone else. There were worse people at my school, so why me? Why was I such a target?

The answer was my insecurity and self-loathing.

As an adult, I can see it clearly now. These kids were merely making up for their own insecurities about themselves. And by making fun of me, no one was making fun of them.

It sucked.

By high school, I wasn't crying every day. Maybe only every other day, or only for a small period each day after school. I had accepted my fate as an outcast and prayed each night for some sort of metamorphosis to take place.

But it never did.

So whereas all my middle school tormentors were now football players and cheerleaders, I was a choir nerd. I was on the honor roll. I was still my teacher's pet.

I believed that I was stronger than the names I was called, and that over time my skin had thickened so that they couldn't hurt me anymore.

Wrong.

"Hey, thunder thighs! When we play softball in PE today, why don't you really play? Don't just stand there. Do something!"

I hated Physical Education most of all. I hated everything about it. The teacher. The kids. The activities. The showers. Coming out of the showers and realizing my clothes were gone, thrown on top of the locker bins. The glaring notice each and every day to my athletic deficiencies. I wasn't a jock. I wasn't trying to get a boy's attention by using my body as a divining rod. So most of the time I just suited up and stood there. Waited until the PE teacher came by and then I pretended to be doing something so I could get my daily grade, and then go back to doing nothing.

But softball was a different game. The PE coach had gone to college on a scholarship, had played semi-pro for a while, and was mean-spirited as they came. In those days, teachers could say things to kids that they can't say today.

I had all but avoided her for a week. We rotated through the various positions on the team and it was now my turn to be catcher.

I hated it.

The pitcher knew how much I hated PE and so he threw the ball as hard as he could each and every time. I prayed for each batter to hit it over the fence, but more often than not, they didn't, and it was up to me to catch it and throw it back.

The ball stung my hand as it hit my glove.

"Can you not throw it so hard?"

The pitcher smiled. I had inadvertently given him his secret desire, which was to bring attention to his powerful pitch.

The next pitch was even harder.

It hit my hand so hard I dropped the ball.

"Pick up the damn ball, Vanessa! Get serious. Let's play!"

I wanted to hit the coach with it, but I aimed it back across home plate.

The third pitch was the hardest yet. It hit high in my glove, right at my thumb joint.

I heard a snap.

"Hey, I think I hurt something!" I cried.

"Quit messing around, Vanessa, or I'm failing you. You're the catcher. Your job is to catch the ball, got it? Now let's go."

And so on we played.

Each pitch I caught sent pain shooting up my arm.

I bit my tongue to fight back the tears.

By the end of the period, my thumb was so swollen my glove wouldn't come off.

"Um, excuse me, Coach? I think I broke my thumb."

"How is that? You never could catch the damn ball!"

"Yeah, I did. You just weren't looking. I did catch it, and I think when I did, something broke."

Eventually one of the snobbiest girls in the class would be asked to carry my clothes and backpack to the nurse's office for me. My glove would have to be cut off and my thumb splinted.

I had indeed broken my thumb.

———————

"Well, when you heard the snap, why didn't you stop playing?"

I didn't even bother to answer the therapist. Had I told the nurse the truth, she probably wouldn't have believed me anyway.

Even now, thinking back on that day my blood boils!

"So how did this make you feel?"

Awful!

Here again was another adult not believing me, not validating what I was trying to tell them. It's like everyone thought I was trying to get out of something by faking it and then once they found out I wasn't, they were mad about it. Like it was somehow my fault that I got hurt.

"So what happened?"

Well, that sidelined me for a while, and then I was made fun of for that.

I sucked as an athlete, and then people thought I was faking my injury so I wouldn't have to suit up, and they were jealous.

I couldn't win with those people.

So I gave up.

I asked my doctor to give me a note to permanently excuse me from PE and he did.

That was my last year in PE.

And then I was made fun of for that.

"Why are *you* so special, Vanessa?" they would say.

While other people were out playing dodgeball, I was being a TA for the nurse, or one of my teachers.

In the eyes of my peers, that made me an even bigger nerd because I was hanging out with grown-ups all the time.

The more my teachers loved me, the more my peers hated me.

What they didn't understand is that I didn't ask for that love. I did what I thought was expected and that was the result.

My peers didn't see it that way.

And every day, in every class, they made my life a living hell.

I think that's why I am the teacher that I am. I know what it's like to be totally ostracized by other people. I find those ugly ducklings in my classes and build them up. I want to give them the self-confidence I never had. Still don't.

In group, we've been talking about forgiving others. I know in our sessions we're supposed to talk about that topic in more detail. I want to do that, but I want to talk about death first.

"Okay. What brings this on?"

Something big happened last week and it's on my mind again.

"You think about death a lot, don't you?"

Death is one of those things that I have thought about for most of my life. I've longed for it. I've read books where people die in them—horrible deaths, usually at the hands of some faceless, unknown killer. And that's okay. It's safe. I don't know those people. I don't really feel bad for them. I just read along until they die, and *then* it's like they take on a new life. It seems like no one really needs to know someone until they've died. Then, in an effort to solve the mystery of their death, their whole life story becomes important: their past, their friends, their interests, their fears. All those things that make us who we are seem to go unnoticed unless we die a tragic death.

But this last week was different.

Death finally had a face, and it scared me.

"Why don't you tell me about that."

Well, two things. One, I came across my first fatality accident last week. Someone lost control of his car, slammed into the guardrail, and had apparently been thrown halfway through the windshield. By the time I was finally able to get around it, the body was draped with a white cloth.

I've thought a lot about that person. Where was he going? What was he listening to on the radio? I want to believe it was a good song, his favorite song, so that he had a happy memory as he died. I wonder what pictures that person had in his wallet and how those people will find out that someone they knew or loved died. For the first time in a long time, I think of death and it makes me sad. I don't feel relieved or cavalier. I feel sad. I feel sad because I can see in my mind the way the body was splayed on the hood of the car, and in my heart I know he had to feel his body going through the windshield. I wonder if he had time to cry out. To cry at all. But you know what makes me the saddest? He died alone. No one was there to hold his hand or tell him that he was loved. He truly left this world alone and I hurt for him.

"I imagine that seeing something like that had to have been traumatic for you. Does it bring up some of your own fears about death? Your own mortality?"

Sure. But you know, there are some things that I believe everyone knows: how to breathe, how to know when they've found true love. Me? I believe I'm going to die early. I don't see myself living beyond fifty, and so I feel an incredible sense of urgency to get as much accomplished in the little time I have as I possibly can.

"Do you think you can control when you die?"

To an extent. But I haven't met many people who have the drive I have—the constant "hurry up before it's too late" mentality that I have. I think most people see themselves living to a very ripe old age, and I don't. Never have.

"You said there were two things that made you start thinking about death. What's the other one?"

My mom tried to kill herself last week. That's why I missed my session.

"I had no idea! Is she okay? What happened?"

She got upset. Something set her off and she left the house. She told my stepfather she was going to the grocery store but never came back. I truly believed something awful had happened to her—that she'd been in an accident or kidnapped or something. It never dawned on me that she would have done something to herself. She was missing for three days before she was found in a hotel room hundreds of miles from home. Again, my heart prepared to say goodbye to her for the last time. It seems like that's all I've been doing with her since I was six years old and she became diabetic.

"I know there are lots of details here that we may get into at another time, but I think you've just touched on something very important here. You said your heart was preparing to say good-bye. Does that mean you feel like you've made a conscious effort to pull away from your mother?"

Without a doubt. I will never forget her lying on the couch not being able to wake up. And now I have another image to add to that one as well: the image of her lying on a hospital gurney with her wrists slit and charcoal running down her chest from them pumping her stomach.

"You sound angry."

My eyes fill with unshed tears.

I *am* angry! I'd just visited with her less than a week before she pulled this stunt.

I can feel my pulse race as my fists clench against my thighs.

There was *nothing* about her demeanor that seemed sad or distraught. In fact, I thought we had a lovely time. And then this!

I can feel a wave of sadness wash to the back of my eyes. I tell myself I will not cry over this anymore, but before I know it, a lone salty drop slides out of my eye and splashes on the top of my hand. Angrily, I use my hand to wipe away a tear from the corner of my other eye.

It makes me really question our relationship. If something is going on with me, my mother expects me to call and tell her about it so she can be there for me. But does she return the favor? No! The next thing I know I'm being called out of school to catch a plane and pray that somehow, someway, my mother will turn up alive.

I want to stand up and pace around the office, to use my hands in a wild display of gestures. In a split second, an image of scissors, sharp and gleaming, pops into my mind. Frantically, I push it away.

"So how does this experience, besides the obvious, connect to this idea of death to you?"

Last week I learned that a person can "die" to another person and still be very much alive. I learned that a part of my heart has closed itself off to my mother forever and I hate it.

I realize for the first time that I've been balancing myself on the edge of the sofa in my therapist's office. Catching her eye, I sense how far forward I am and nervously push myself back into the pillows. My eyes close.

The silence in the room prompts me to continue.

Seeing my mother and what she'd done to herself, I don't think I've ever been so angry in all of my life.

Another tear springs forth and I hastily brush it away. Then another. And another. Clenching my fists, I hit my thighs while trying to mentally put the lid back on the flow of emotions swelling from my heart.

"Angry at what?"

Breathing deeply, I try to bore a hole into the wall with my eyes. My voice sounds distant and defeated.

That somehow trying to kill herself was a better choice than asking for help, reaching out to her children, talking to my stepfather, anything! And you know the worst of it? I've spent a week feeling completely worthless and guilty because I wasn't able to rescue her from herself.

My palms are imprinted with nail marks. I hadn't realized I was clenching my fists so tightly. I open my hands and rub them across my thighs, trying to make the marks disappear.

"That's the problem, isn't it? You can't save another person from themselves. Is there a part of *you* that wants to be saved? Is that what your cuts are? Cries for help?"

I am speechless.

I turn and face my therapist, mouth agape and eyes wide open. My heart feels like it's stopping, one tenuous beat at a time.

I'm not breathing. To do so would mean I had the means to answer. The implication of the question is too much. I keep talking.

A shallow breath and, again, an image of scissors pops into my mind. For a split second, I imagine what they would feel like in my hands at this moment. Cold. Heavy. Comfortable. In a panic, I push the image away a second time. I tell myself I have to work through these feelings; I can't just run headlong into physical pain anymore to escape.

I continue the story.

At one point, a nurse came in to change the dressings on her wrists, and for the first time, I saw the severity of the cuts she'd made. I kept asking her why she did it. My heart hurt for her.

I start to massage my temples. The stress of reliving this event and fighting the call of the scissors is too much and pressure has started to build behind my eyes.

For the first time in my life, I cried for *my* scars. I realized at that very moment how much it must hurt other people when I cut myself. I never knew how awful that felt until I saw what my mother had done to herself out of anger and self-loathing.

"Do you think there is an element of selfishness then to your injuring yourself? If you felt that way looking at your mother's cuts, do you think others feel the same way when they see yours?"

I don't cut myself in an attempt to die! It's not the same thing! The feelings behind my scars are totally different. And to tell you the truth, I don't really think people pay that much attention or give it a second thought. They have their own lives and they deal with their feelings in their own way.

"Vanessa. Take a moment here and look at your scars. Tell me what you think when you see them."

I look down to my lap expecting to see my wrists and arms and realize that they aren't there. At some point I had put myself in a bear hug, but I don't remember doing it. Trying to unknot my arms feels like moving in quicksand. The pressure behind my eyes is getting worse.

Finally, my eyes find what they're looking for. A series of triangles etched into my wrist. Several deep scars running along the bones of my arms. I look at them and feel nothing.

"Well? What are you thinking?"

I'm thinking that I did this. I look at these lines and shapes as battle scars—necessary sacrifices for the greater good. I'm here talking to you today because I did this. I really believe had I not cut, I would have died. The feelings I had while doing this were so intense that they would have overpowered me. In my mind it was a choice. Cut or die. It's that easy.

Part of me thinks you are expecting me to be ashamed of them, but I'm not. Or maybe you're expecting me to say I regret making them. But I don't.

I run my index finger along each scar gingerly.

If I think hard enough, I can remember exactly where I was, how old I was, and what I was going through when I made each cut. Some have a person's name associated with them. Others just an event. I am the only constant—the only thing that doesn't change. I was present when each cut was made. In a weird way, that's comforting to me to know that I had control over each of these marks. No one else. I didn't get them in an accident. I didn't get them from an abusive boyfriend. I gave each one of these to myself.

"What do you think your mother will think of now when she sees her scars?"

I stick my hands under my thighs to keep them still.

I imagine she will regret them. I don't know that she realizes how angry her family is at her yet. But once she does, I think that her scars will remind her of that anger and it will be something that she tries to forget.

"You never did answer my question about *your* scars as being a possible cry for help. Could they be?"

I feel the bottom fall out of my stomach. I yank my hands out from under my thighs and start to rub each one of my fingers as I talk. If I'm lucky, I can find a hangnail I can work on. Pain. Big pain. Small pain. Any pain has to be better than this.

I think this is a loaded question. If I say yes, then I cut for attention. If I say no, then I don't expect anyone to react to the marks I've made.

For me, my scars aren't absolutes. At one time, yeah, maybe they were a cry for help. Maybe part of me believed that if I was hurting enough and people could see that hurt, they would intervene on my behalf and try to take the pain away. This makes sense to me because I feel so childlike sometimes when I cut. Maybe there is a part of me that wants another person to be parent-like and stop me. Wrap me in their arms, let me cry, and then reassure me that it's going to be okay. But it's *never* okay! Or at least they could offer to talk to me about my scars openly. But I've learned that will never happen. People don't see my scars and want to help. They recoil in horror. They say things like, "How could you do that?" or "You're so beautiful. Why do you want to make yourself ugly?" or "Can't you find a better way to communicate?"

"So, if someone asks you, you tell them you made them your-self?"

Depends on the person asking. If it's someone who has no idea that I self-injure, then no, I usually give them one of my pat excuses, they believe it, and then move on. Other people who are closer to me will ask more questions about the pat excuse they're given and slowly unravel the lie. Other people know I self-injure. So if they see something new, they know where it came from. Regardless, no one understands it. And because inflicting pain on yourself is so foreign to the whole human makeup, it scares people and creates distance in the relationship. Now my mother and I have something else between us to create distance. I don't want my mother to *ever* think that the attention she received with her suicide attempt is in any way a kind of attention I want.

"You said you wished you could have saved your mother from herself. What does that mean?"

If I could have known what she was going to do, I would have gone to the ends of the earth to stop her. I would have taken her car keys and all her money. I would have physically wrestled her down if I had to in order to stop her from hurting herself. I would have told anyone I could so they could help me. I would have had her committed. Anything to stop her from putting our family through what she has.

"Let's say you did all of that and then once you were gone, because you can't be by her side forever, she does it anyway. Just because the timing is off doesn't mean the desire goes away. You should know that. Is there anything in the world that your husband, your friends, your family members, or me could do to stop you from hurting yourself once you've decided that's what you're going to do?"

I look at her incredulously.

No! Because by the time that decision has been made, I am no longer thinking rationally. The time to intervene is before that when there is still time . . . when there is still a chance to silence the voices . . . to reach out to the part of me that feels like it has no other choice!

"Look at what you're asking here. People can't read your mind.

How do they know when you're about to cross that line? Today you may be fine but tomorrow you may not be. If you don't tell people, they aren't going to know. If you really want help, then you have to help yourself by communicating your needs to the people in your life."

I don't know how.

My fingers have found a stray cuticle edge and are working it over painfully.

"Yes, you do. The problem is you don't think you are worth the time and attention you crave from other people."

My eyes harden. My cuticle, sticky with blood, pulsates rhythmically. The feeling of relief has been lost because my mind cannot escape with the pain.

Look. For as long as I can remember, I've wanted to die. As a child, I prayed that God would take me away and send my parents the kind of child they deserved—a better child, a perfect child. I prayed for a disease or an accident. Something that would release my parents from the burden that I believed myself to be.

I never imagined that my mother might have those same feelings. Maybe she does. Maybe with all her health problems she feels like a burden to us. I never believed she would understand my not wanting to be on this earth anymore, and so I kept her from all those thoughts in my heart. I thought it would hurt her to know that I wanted to give back the greatest gift she ever gave me, my life.

But her thoughts were imprinted, permanently, on her body, just as so many of my feelings are.

I had always believed that my death would be a relief for people—that they would mourn me for a couple weeks and then move on, grateful to be rid of a problem.

But seeing my mom lying there, I realized how wrong I was in that thinking. If I were to die, especially by my own hand, I would devastate those closest to me. The only person who would benefit by my death would be me, and that would make me a worse person. A selfish one.

"It sounds like for the first time in a long time you and your mother are on the same page. Can you not use this experience to bridge a gap between you? Can you not reach out to her as someone who understands very well the pain she may be going through?"

No. When I cut, it is never with the intention of ending my life. I have always believed I would die early, true. But not by my own hand. When I cut, no one else is impacted in any way. They may feel sorry for me, but that's all. I hate my mother for what she tried to do. I think of how many years she has fought diabetes so that she could see her children grow up, get married, have children. Regardless of what else happened in my life I knew that my mother was there, fighting for one more day with me. Last week, she tried to give up that fight and I can't forgive her for that. I want her to keep fighting. I want her to stick around long enough to see me do something wonderful! Maybe then she can forgive me for not being the daughter she always thought she would have. I never found value in the skills she had and wanted to teach me. Her dream of being able to impart to me some of her wisdom died a long time ago. The least I can do for her is to show her that by sacrificing her dream, she allowed me to fulfill mine. If I share some of my happiness with her, then maybe she will forgive me for taking away some of her own.

"So how can someone die and be alive?"

In the days that she was missing, I was so worried for her before I knew what she'd tried to do. A million thoughts went through my mind: kidnapping, murder, rape, fatal car accident, drive-by shooting. I really believed that if there was any way for my mother to fight and stay alive, she would. How devastating to know that wasn't the case.

Over the past twenty-five years or so, I think I have been mentally preparing for a final good-bye. There have been many times over the years when she has nearly died and each one has been more painful than anything else I've ever experienced. With each near miss, my heart has died a little more so that when the next time comes, I'm steeled against the pain. It has been years since my mother and I have been close. I can't let that happen because I know the second I let her back into my heart, she will leave me again, maybe permanently, and I will be devastated. I feel like I have loved my mother fully. I have mourned her fully. You can't mourn someone that intensely over and over again without becoming numb. Last week was so emotionally taxing that I don't think I could ever feel that way again, even if she were to die. It's like, in my heart, I've already said good-bye, buried her, and moved on. When she really dies, I can't imagine mourning her anymore.

"That sounds painful. Have you thought about how your pulling away from your mother, regardless of your reasons, may have affected her? Made her feel inadequate as a parent? You said you felt guilty for not being able to save her. Perhaps she feels equally guilty for not being able to save you."

That could be. But I still don't think I am in a place where I could talk to her about this. I am way too angry to be so vulnerable right now. Plus, I don't know that my mom is ready to hear what I have to say. I needed certain things from her at different times in my life. Some of those things I got; others I didn't. I can't help but mourn those things missing in my life.

I believe it is important for me to always tell my mother that I love her and appreciate her in my life each time we talk, and I do. That's all she needs to know. The rest is too complicated and will bring up more questions than we may have time to answer. I don't want her to ever feel like there were unresolved issues between us, so I don't bring them up. My mother knows I have pulled away; I'm sure she can sense it. If she wanted to know why or work to change it, she would approach me about it and she hasn't. I think that may be for the best.

"Maybe she hasn't approached you because, like you say, there may be too many questions and too little time for answers. Your mother has a disease that is robbing her of time. Maybe she wants to spend the time she has with you on happier, and in her mind, more productive things."

Okay. I get that. But a larger part of me feels that long after she's gone, I'll still be dealing with these things. It is hard for me to focus on anything else right now. Once I answer some things for myself, then perhaps I'll have the mental energy to devote to other issues. But for now, I have to try to understand why I am the way I am. Period.

"So what do you need to do?"

I have to learn to forgive her for what she tried to do. Although I understand the feelings behind it, I can't get past her acting on those thoughts. I can't get past her thinking that somehow my life would be better without her in it. If she only knew how many times I have wanted to kill myself. But I didn't want to make her life more difficult. I expected the same commitment from her and I didn't get it. Now I don't know where we stand. Maybe she is sad she failed. Maybe she will try again. I don't know that I am strong enough to handle either of these possibilities.

"So, what has changed for you over the last week?"

I wish I could say that I don't want to die anymore, but that would be untrue. There are times when I feel so bad about the things I've done or failed to do that death seems like the only redemption available to me. But my attitude toward death has changed in that I know now that it will affect people who know me in ways I can't possibly imagine, and that makes me sad. But part of what made this thing with my mom so frightening is that I kept thinking about the void her death would create in my life, and because we'd never talked about her death and what her desires were, if I did the "wrong thing" I might be a disappointment to her again, even in the afterlife. This got me to thinking about my life and death, so I've decided to take matters into my own hands and make sure that people around me know what I want so they don't feel that same responsibility.

"Wow. You've really been doing some thinking. So, what are you going to do with this?"

I've made an appointment with my attorney. My husband and I are going to fill out our living wills and all the other stuff that goes along with it. I don't want there to be a great expense for my family after I die. I want my organs to go to whoever can use them. I want to make my passing as easy as possible for other people, and this is a way I can do that.

"Do you think you're going to die?"

Yes.

"Are you thinking about taking that decision into your own hands?"

No.

I have no doubt I am going to die. Part of me believes that if I don't get this damn cutting thing fixed I may end up killing myself by accident. But if I did, it truly would be an accident. I don't want to go out of this world covered in shit because I couldn't cope. When it's my time, it will be my time. I just want to be ready.

"So, how is the medication coming?"

Fine.

"No, really. Can you tell any difference?"

Yes. Some days more than others, but I can tell that I'm a little more even now. It's like I can think more clearly. You don't know how much I hate admitting that to you. I didn't want you to be right.

"Yes, I know. But this isn't about me being right. It's about you feeling better and getting stronger."

I don't want to be on these pills for the rest of my life.

"No one said you had to be. But I think for right now, it's important. How much are you taking?"

The doctor has started me off on a low dosage and then wants me to work my way up.

"I think that's good. Your body has to slowly build up the chemicals in your body. If you did it all at once, it wouldn't be healthy."

So, if I have to work my way up, do I have to work my way down, too? I'm looking ahead. I'm thinking I want to go cold turkey off these things the second I get this cutting thing under control. I'm not a medication person and I hate that I'm so weak emotionally that this is where I am. I should be stronger than this. I feel like these stupid pills are just a crutch.

"Vanessa. Whom exactly are you comparing yourself to? This is not a competition. This is now and has always been about you. You are dealing with some very difficult emotional issues and the feelings you are experiencing are manifesting themselves in unhealthy ways. In order to even you out a little bit, I recommended you go on antidepressants so you don't get halfway through this process and either shut down on me completely because it's too painful or end up becoming so overwhelmed your cutting gets out of control. At this time, you need something to take the edge off the power of your emotions a little bit. That's all. This is not a comment on the strength of your character or a life sentence that says you have to take these pills forever. But for now, they are a critical component of your re-covery, and that's how you have to see them."

Part of me knows that and wants the pills to work. I want the edge to be taken off a little bit because, more often than not, the feelings are too strong and I can't control them. But I feel like that's part of why I'm here. If I'm not going to take medication for the rest of my life, then I have to learn how to deal with these feelings. They're going to come back, sooner or later, and I have to be ready.

"I agree, Vanessa, but look at what you're doing. As always, you're looking ahead and missing the present. You need to be most con-cerned with right now. Over time, you will develop the skills you need to better deal with your feelings and the events of your past. I don't know how long that will take. So let's take this one step at a time. We're here today, right now, and that's all we can worry about. Now, if I'd been seeing you for ten years and you weren't making progress, that would be another issue. But that hasn't happened. Is it slow going? You betcha. We all wish we could hurry up the healing process. But we can't. You and I have to take this journey together, one step at a time, with the common goal of you becoming a stronger and more emotionally stable individual. Your job is to trust me—to know that I have worked with enough people with similar back-grounds, to know that what you're feeling is normal and appropriate. Unless you announce to the world that you are on antidepressants, no one should be able to tell. Your taking medication doesn't dimin-ish any of the professional or personal accomplishments you have. It is merely a small piece of a larger process. But in the end, it's your choice. I cannot make you take your meds. I cannot make you eat. I cannot make you stop cutting. But I can work with you and help you to establish a healthy emotional framework in which you can live. So, what do you want to do?"

Silence.

My palms itch from the nail marks I have repeatedly dug into them.

The voices start their mantra. You're weak . . . Weak! . . . WEAK!

Why does everything have to be so freakin' difficult?

"I've learned that most of the time it isn't the thing that is difficult;

it's our attitude about it. No one ever said this would be easy, Vanessa. You have to give yourself time and patience. I've said this to you before. You didn't get this way overnight, and you won't magically change overnight either. That has nothing to do with you. That's just the way it is."

Um . . . I've also been thinking about something else.

"What is that?"

I've decided that I don't want to leave any loose ends behind when I die. Part of me really believes that things that I don't deal with in this life will await me in the next one. I don't want that. I want to deal with everything here, now, so I can move past them.

"I think you are. I mean, you've come a long way in group, and you seem to be more focused here in our sessions. I definitely think you're making progress."

No, you don't get it. I think the only way I'm going to be able to move on is if I do something that we haven't really talked about in here before.

"Like what?"

I haven't said anything because I think you're going to try to talk me out of it. But I think this is something I have to do. It's time. I'm ready.

"What is it?"

I need to contact my dad. I need to see if he's still around and curious about what has happened in my life.

Finally, the tears come.

I've thought about this for so long. Part of me is ready to go and the other part of me is scared shitless. I mean, what if I reach out to him and get nothing back? I want to say it wouldn't matter, but it does matter.

"Vanessa, I am here to support you. You know how I feel about you moving so fast. I'm not sure you're as ready as you think you are. If he rejects you again, how will that make you feel? How will that affect what you're trying to do? I want to help you see that you don't need him or his approval to move on in your life. *You* have all of the answers you'll ever need; you just don't know it yet."

I have to do this.

"Can I ask you to wait for a couple more months? Let us work through some more things in group before you try?"

No. I think I'm ready now.

The counselor's eyes fall to her lap.

"All right. If you want to do this, let's at least talk through it a time or two."

Good. Now here's what I want to do. . . .

There are some things in life that are impossible: licking your elbow, keeping your eyes open when you sneeze, knowing the second you fall asleep. Impossible, but once we hear about them, we have to try them anyway. There's something about me that's like that. If I hear something can't be done, I try it. And then if I fail, I beat myself up over it. I can accept that other people can't do something, but for me to accept that of myself is almost too much.

In a literal sense, my parents came from poor white-trash families. My grandparents were cotton farmers, and so most of their understanding of the world stemmed from their limited small-town farm experiences. It was hard for them to understand that not all Mexicans were poor and ignorant or in this country illegally. African Americans were seen as "help," and the idea that my parents would grow up to be anything that they weren't already was incomprehensible.

As a result, my parents created an artificial "we are better than that" type of mentality at home. As children, we were discouraged from pursuing anything that might be seen by outsiders as "trashy" or "low class," such as comic books, cheesy movies, fast food, certain clothes or makeup, and amusement parks.

In an effort to be better than their poor white-trash upbringing, the pursuance of education and all of the accessories that go along with education—such as museums, nonfiction literature, live theatre, classic literature, lectures, foreign film series, zoos, musical concerts, and aquariums—were deemed to be most *important. Anything outside of this realm was considered trivial and unimportant, regardless of how fun it might be.*

As a child, I didn't care about being well read and cultural. I wanted to have fun. I enjoyed reading mystery novels and watching Disney movies. My television privileges were closely monitored and limited to about one hour per day. I usually had my choice: Little House on the Prairie *or something on PBS. Only in rare instances would I be allowed to see both.*

A part of myself fractured off as a child because, here again, the things that I valued and thought were important were deemed unacceptable. For example, my birthday is in July. As a result, most of my friends were never around to attend a birthday party. In the third grade, I begged my parents to let me celebrate my birthday early, before the end of the school year, so I could actually have my friends attend. In my mind, I was thinking of a piñata, party hats, and cake. Oh no. That's what a poor, white-trash child would have. My parents went out and rented a reel-to-reel machine and hung a white curtain on the living room wall so that my friends and I could watch educational movies about baby tigers. I wanted to die. My friends hated my party and wanted to leave early. My parents were angry that my friends weren't paying closer attention. And I was told that I couldn't hang out with a couple of them anymore because they weren't good enough for me. That was the last time I ever asked for a birthday party.

In the sixth grade, my class took a field trip to the Seattle Center. This is a hands-on museum with dinosaurs, space exhibits, and Indian longhouses inside. There is an IMAX building and a larger building that houses the food court and specialty shops. On the outside is a huge carnival area.

I loved the Seattle Center. I loved that the museum was hands-on because it made learning fun. My parents got us a membership when we moved to Seattle, and so I went there on a fairly regular basis. When my class went there on a field trip, my peers were thrilled because many of them had never been before. But you know how sixth-graders are. Their parents send them on a field trip with a pocketful of money, a sack lunch, and a free spirit. Once we arrived, the museum was dismissed and the carnival became the focus of attention. But not for me. Because, you see, I had been taught that carnivals were low class and dangerous. I was told that only poor, uneducated saps would spend their hard-earned money on cheesy rides and not the more educational exhibits. And I knew if I went on one ride, I would let my parents down in a way I couldn't possibly imagine.

And so I walked. And walked. And walked. And walked some more. I told myself it didn't matter, that I really didn't want to go on any of those stupid rides anyway, and I desperately tried to block out the joyous screams of my classmates as they went on one ride after another. Always the little adult, I went into the Seattle Center and ate lunch by myself. Unlike my peers, I hadn't thrown my brown-bag lunch away. So, I sat there, at a table by myself, and berated myself for being so weak as to want to have fun like my friends. Adults, I told myself, didn't need carnival rides to have fun. A real adult could be entertained with something more cultural and refined.

After lunch I started walking again until I found a sticker store. This was a middle ground. It wasn't cheesy like the carnival rides, but stickers could be fun. I spent over an hour in that store looking for just the right addition to my collection. Finally, I settled on a Boynton sticker with sheep on a tropical island. It said, "Isle of Ewe." I was so proud of myself! Yes, I had gone into a sticker store, but I had found one that was a play on words. Surely my parents wouldn't be mad at me if I bought it! So I pulled out my dollar; collected my change and small, white plastic bag; and went outside to try, again, to ignore the screams of my friends as they went on the rides over and over again. My heart longed to join them, but when I thought about the disappointment my parents would feel in me if I did, I closed the door on that desire. I told myself I didn't really want to go on the "stupid" roller coaster and continued to walk around the exhibits, alone.

As I grew older, I decided that I didn't need my parents' approval on certain things anymore, and riding a roller coaster was one of them. I decided to branch out and give myself permission to do what I wanted to do. I learned to enjoy some things just because they made me happy, and not worry about what other people would think about me doing them. I think this is why I love Disney World so much and go there as often as I can. I think a part of me feels like I'm getting away with something. I've got my two college degrees, I'm established in my career, and so I've finally earned the right to have fun that isn't educational in nature. I can't tell you what a thrill that is! When I go to Florida, I'm not learning anything on purpose. I ride the rides for the sake of riding the rides, and it's fantastic!

My parents always let my brothers and I know what was expected of us from day one. There was no second-guessing their expectations. Rules were rules were rules, regardless of where you were and who you were with.

The idea of doing the right thing even when no one else is looking has been a moral compass my entire life. I have never been able to shut it off or ignore it, even in instances when I could probably have done something and gotten away with it. It has complicated my life in ways you could never imagine, because it has forced me, more often than not, to leave the herd and go off by myself in order to remain true to this moral code.

My parents never *let us watch R-rated movies. Period. If something came on the television that was a little too adult, my brothers and I were dismissed from the family room. Movies with an R rating were presented in a way that left me feeling that they were "nasty" and "sex filled" and completely "trashy." In my little adolescent brain, I believed it to be true.*

In high school, I was the antithesis of popularity. Invitations to sleepovers were few and far between, and so this privilege that I had begged and cried so long for seemed completely empty. I mean, what good is a privilege if the oppor-tunity never arises when you can exercise it? In the ninth grade, I finally had a chance to attend a birthday party sleepover at a friend's house. My mother had called to make sure the girl's parents would be home, and I was sent off with a litany of reminders about appropriate ladylike behavior, sanitation, and our house rules. On this occasion, the birthday girl's parents had rented Flash Dance *for us to watch. I had heard so much about this movie, I couldn't wait! I had been wearing the latest in* Flash Dance *fashions for months: leg warmers, off-the-shoulder sweatshirt, and bows. Finally, I would have a chance to see where these fashions had come from! I asked someone to pass me the movie box. I wanted to look at the beautiful girl on the cover. And that's when I saw the sticker from the rental place: rated R.*

I handed the box back and desperately tried to think of some reason I could use to leave the family room while they watched the movie. I hadn't brought a book and I couldn't call home. If I did call to ask permission, my mother would come get me immediately. I was stuck. Rules were rules were rules, regardless of where I was or who I was with. And so I waited until the girls turned off the lights and I snuck out of the room. I sat, for over two hours, in the laundry room. I counted ceiling tiles. Floor tiles. Dead bugs. Lint balls. Anything to pass the time. After about an hour, another girl came into the laundry room looking for me. I couldn't tell her about "the rules," so I lied and told her the pizza wasn't agreeing with me. She had already seen the movie "a thousand times" and so she sat in the laundry room with me until it was over. I wanted to die.

Once the movie was over and I could come out of hiding, I went about the same drill as I had in the past of setting up my sleeping bag. The entire conver-

sation was about this movie and I felt totally left out. I put my sleeping bag in the corner and cried myself to sleep.

I hated myself for being so disciplined over stupid stuff and I hated my friends for not being sensitive enough to see my shoulders rise and fall with each sob. And most of all, I hated my parents for not being able to see how good I really was. I was a total fuck up at home. But when they weren't looking, I really did try to be the best I could be for them. In my mind, if I died, my friends could tell my parents, "No, she didn't watch the movie" or "No, she never rode any of those carnival rides," and they would be pleased. That's all I've ever wanted was for my parents to be pleased. I guess that's part of my problem.

———————

"So, Vanessa, how do you feel if you aren't doing the right thing?"

Awful. Like a complete disappointment. Like a failure.

"Why didn't you ever tell your parents about your discipline? I'm sure they would have been very proud of you."

They wouldn't have believed me. I mean, I had no proof I had done the right thing. Without proof, my words are hollow, so I kept them to myself.

"Why do you need proof?"

Because I am not a credible source. My entire life has been spent collecting proof for my case that I really am a good person.

"Like what?"

Like straight As on my report card. If my parents asked about how I did on a test and I said fine, they wanted to see the paper. If they looked at the paper and didn't agree with my assessment of "fine," then I was a liar and my word was invalid. But, if they saw the paper and saw that it had a good grade on it, then my assessment of "fine" was validated.

My whole life has been like this.

"What do you mean?"

No one believes me unless I have something tangible to back up what I say. If I say, "I used to play the piano," people come back with, "Perhaps you can play me something sometime." It's like they won't believe I really did that unless they see and hear me for themselves. If I say, "I studied French in school," people say, "Really? For how long? Say something in French." My word isn't good enough. It never has been.

"I think you're selling yourself short."

No, I'm not. You did it to me too. When I came in here the first day, I told you I cut myself. You didn't believe me. You weren't willing to take me at my word. You didn't even believe me when I showed you the bandages! No, you had to see what was *under* them to know if I was telling you the truth or not. I'm telling you, my words mean *nothing!* They never have.

"Vanessa, when I asked to see what was under your bandages, I didn't doubt you. I needed to see what you were talking about. I needed to know how severe of a problem this is for you."

Whatever.

You needed proof. That's all my life is . . . collecting proof that I am a good person, a committed member of the community, and a consummate professional so that when I die, people will be able to say, "Well, damn. Vanessa was telling the truth. She really was all these things, and here are notebooks and notebooks filled with certificates and letters and awards to prove it."

"Vanessa, are you sure you aren't rationalizing here? I mean, *you* are the one who needs those things. Do you really think the world cares if you have one degree or two? Three national teaching awards or ten? After a certain point it becomes moot. *You* are the reason the world knows you are a good person. Your personality, your kind heart, your spirit. Not the things you do or the awards you win."

Not true. How many so-called good people are there in this world? I mean really, honest-to-God good people? Not many. How does someone know you are a good person if they don't know you? By what others have said about you. I can't take a notebook filled with endorsements with me wherever I go. So I have the next best thing. Letters after my name. Pages of accomplishments on a résumé. *Those* are the things that are my endorsements. And I have to keep acquiring them. Why? Because if I don't, then it means I *was* a good person, but then something happened and the endorsements stopped, so maybe I'm not such a good person anymore.

"Vanessa, why do you connect who you are with what you do? They are totally different parts of yourself."

We've gone over and over this. I *have* to be perfect! The world won't like me if I'm not!

The tears fall onto my lap.

"But you can never *be* perfect!"

But the fact that I even have that desire says a lot about me, doesn't it? Most people aren't that disciplined or focused. But I am. I have the endurance to run the race and the focus to get all the prizes along the way. I want to prove to the world that just because I like to have fun, it doesn't mean I can't be a good person! I don't want people to see me reading for pleasure or yelling at the top of my lungs as I go down a roller coaster and think that I'm trashy. I'm not! I'm better than the selfish desires in my heart. I can be better than the people around me who spend their time watching television and reading romance novels. The world needs me to be better than that. My *parents* need me to be better than that.

"Vanessa, when will you decide that you've done enough? Your parents *have* to be proud of you by now."

But it's only temporary. It's only until I can accomplish the next big thing. Otherwise, I'm stagnant.

"Vanessa, you push yourself harder than anyone I've met in a long time. Other people look up to you. You have walls filled with plaques and newspaper articles and diplomas. You *are* a good person!"

The tissue I have in my hands has been reduced to shreds.

Then why do the voices in my head tell me otherwise? Why do they tell me what a disappointment I am? Why, when I look in the mirror, do I see someone who is undisciplined and unfocused? Why do I see someone who isn't perfect?

"Because you aren't perfect. Your perspective is way off here. There are not a lot of people who would be willing to do what you do because it makes life drudgery, no fun. Is your life fun, Vanessa?"

My response comes out in a whisper.

No.

"Why not?"

Because well-educated people don't have fun. They don't like riding rides, reading books for fun, or seeing cheesy movies. But I *do* like those things. But that makes me like everyone else, right? So it has to be bad. My parents expect me to be better than that. Taking trips to the Grand Canyon instead of Las Vegas. Going to a museum instead of a pizza place. Reading the greatest works of O. Henry at night instead of the latest James Patterson novel. I feel like I'm being ripped in half! I want to make other people happy, but I want to be happy, too. I don't think there is any way for that to happen, and so I focus more on what others want than what I want. Because if I focus on what *I* want, then that really does make me selfish, doesn't it? Then those things my dad said about me all those years ago really would be true. *It isn't true!*

"I know."

You couldn't know! You don't know anything about me other than what I tell you.

My breath comes in shallow gasps.

"Vanessa. Most of the time when we are talking, you are talking about what others expect and want from you. What do you want for yourself?"

That's irrelevant. I'm not supposed to have needs because that makes me selfish, right?

"Not necessarily. You have needs just like anyone else and you need to listen to those. You almost died over the holidays because you didn't listen to what your body needed. Your body is covered with scars because you didn't listen to what your mind needed. Listen. Be fair. If other people can tell you what they need, then you should be able to tell them what *you* need."

But if I don't have needs, that makes me better than them.

"No, it doesn't. It makes people around you feel bad. It makes them look weak next to you and it damages the relationship. Be open and honest with people. If you're sad, then you have to tell them,

'Hey, I could really use a friend right now.' They would probably love to know that they are needed."

But if I open myself to needing other people, I am going to be disappointed. I have been my whole life.

"So try again. Yeah, people will disappoint you, but you have to keep trying. Don't give up on yourself. Haven't you ever been shopping and found exactly what you wanted but it wasn't in your size? Do you just go home and forget it? Or, do you drive to another store to see if they have it? That's what you have to do. Keep looking. Find someone who you can be really open and honest with and try it."

You would think I could be that way with my husband.

"Yes, I would. But if you don't know how to voice your needs, then it isn't a surprise that your husband is as much in the dark as everyone else. He's flying blind. Give him something to go on. *Trust him.*"

I look down at my lap and the hundreds of tissue fibers that lie there.

But what if I make myself vulnerable to him and he laughs? Or decides he can't do what I need him to do? Then what?

"Then you cross that bridge when you get to it. Bring him in with you sometime and let's role-play. Give him a chance to be the person you need him to be. Don't automatically assume that he isn't capable of being there for you. That's not fair."

I think I need to go away for a while.

"Why?"

Because I need to know who I am. I thought I knew, but now I'm not so sure anymore.

"Where would you go?"

Away.

"Away where?"

Someplace far, far away where no one knows me or my problems.

"Running away isn't going to solve anything. You have to face this or else you'll be dealing with these issues forever."

I'm done. I don't have the energy to keep going over these

memories and trying to make sense of them all. Maybe I'm beyond help.

"I disagree. I think we're finally reaching a critical point in your therapy and it makes you uncomfortable and you want to stop. What are you so afraid of?"

The tears start up again.

I don't know.

"Yes, I think you do."

NO, I DON'T!

"Where is this anger coming from, Vanessa? Tell me."

I avert my eyes so I can look out the window. I find a bird sitting outside and will myself into its body.

"Vanessa, you're clenching your teeth. What are you so *afraid* of?"

Nothing.

"Don't shut down on me, Vanessa. Be honest. You've done great today. Tell me what you're afraid of."

Feeling this alone my whole life. Feeling like everyone around me has the freedom to be happy and carefree while I have to be responsible and "better than that." I don't want to be "better than that"! I want to be silly and stupid and carefree for once in my life. I have had only one drink in my life. One! Why? Because people who drink are undisciplined and trashy! I want to pay eight dollars to go see a movie that has no higher-level message or cultural implication in it. I want to laugh at people doing stupid things and not feel guilty about it! I want to go on vacation and have fun. I don't want to have to feel like if there is a choice between Knottsberry Farm and a string museum that I'm white trash because I want to ride a goddamned roller coaster! I don't want to feel like I have to spend my whole life proving to the world that I'm a good person. I want my word to be good enough. I want to get off this gerbil wheel my life has become, but I don't know how.

I'm exhausted.

I want to reach for another tissue, but all life has left my body. My eyes are closed and my palms are red from nail marks. If I could, I would lie down and take a nap.

"Vanessa, I have something I'd like you to do for me. "

Great. Now I'm so pathetic I need my *own* assignment.

"It's not an assignment."

Fine! What is it?

"I want you to go home and tell your husband to take you to an amusement park this weekend. Let him plan it out. When you go, where you park, what rides you do first. Turn over the control to someone else for a while and see what happens. I want you to eat something totally for fun—a funnel cake or an ice cream. See one of their shows. Laugh at the characters and their antics. Go and enjoy. Tell your husband that this is something I've asked you to do, and let him help you with it. Have fun together. Laugh. Ride. Let the heaviness in your heart go for a little while. It will be there waiting for you when you're ready for it. But let it go. Prove to yourself that your life isn't drudgery. Go, and enjoy."

But I am supposed to do something else this weekend.

"Is it work related?"

Yes.

"If it's something that you *have* to do, do it. But if it's not, and you can get away with calling in sick, do. Your heart needs some attention right now and work isn't cutting it."

I feel totally defeated. I want to go and have fun, but that's not what a responsible person would do. I'm torn.

"Are you going to go?"

I don't know.

"You need to decide before you leave this office. Otherwise, I have no doubt that you won't go. *Go!*"

I don't want others to think I'm a slacker.

"Who cares? This is *one* weekend. Just for you. You said you were committed to getting better, right? Well, I think this is important."

Okay. I'll go.

"What?"

I'll go.

"I want to really hear you say it."

I'LL GO!

I smile.

"Are you excited?"

Yes.

"No, are you excited?"

YES!

"Great. I'll see you in a couple days."

I hate to admit how much fun I had that day riding the roller coasters with my husband. It had been a long time since I'd felt so free. Wind in my hair, white knuckles clenched on the lap bar, eyes closed as I felt the air leave my lungs as I crested over the first and biggest hill. My heart raced, not out of fear, but out of exhilaration. It was fantastic! By the time we got home, our skin was sticky with sweat and our clothes marred by dirt. My ponytail, hours old, had given way to a myriad of tendrils that framed my face. My reflective sunglasses left me with raccoon eyes when I took them off, and for the first time in a long time, I didn't care. For one day, I hadn't worried about money, unfulfilled expectations, or impressing someone else. Somehow, over the course of several hours, my soul had healed a little.

———————

Once in a while, someone comes into your life who teaches you a lesson in a way you could have never predicted. The first person to teach me such a lesson was Anna, a student in my sixth-grade English class. She had leukemia and died within weeks of my first meeting her. But in our few brief interactions with each other, I learned that a person's attitude on the inside has a lot to do with his or her attitude on the outside. Even though she knew she was dying, she was one of the most positive people I have ever met. She fought her disease valiantly and with more grace than I imagined possible.

The second was a girl named Laura. When I close my eyes and picture her, more often than not, I envision her and me together—a pair of misfits in a freshman gym class filled with athletes and letterman-jacket contenders. With bright red hair and whorish pink lipstick, her overweight frame seemed to attract whatever ridicule my scrawny body deflected. We were an odd pairing, and whenever I see her in my mind, I still see her with a red T-shirt and purple, tight-fitting sweatpants. When we ran laps around the track, we would tie for last place. She, because she couldn't run any faster, I, because I didn't want to.

We were usually the last to be chosen for team sports and used our time out in the field to laugh at our peers who believed that sports were life and that without them the earth would cease rotation. But as with most lessons in life, they usually occur when we least expect it. Laura's lesson was no different.

I can see her there, hair blowing crazily in the wind, and lipstick congealed in the corners of her mouth. I can see her smile, crooked teeth with a slight yellowish tartar tinge. She is frozen in my mind that way, forever.

As we left for Thanksgiving holidays, we told each other good-bye. I was leaving for Hawaii and she was leaving for eastern Washington. It was the last time I would ever see her, for on her way east, she would meet a man on the bus who would follow her home and then chop her up into pieces, stuff her in a closet, and leave her there, unnoticed, until the smell of decaying flesh would prompt neighbors to call the police.

Even now, twenty years later, her death seems surreal. To think that her vivacity and good-hearted laugh were silenced in such a tremendously brutal way is almost more than I can bear. It was the first time in my life I had been met with the very real possibility of dying at the hands of another person.

In the days and weeks that followed, I cried for her—for the pain she surely suffered, the family she left behind, the children she would never have, the potential she would never realize. And I resolved to be all that I could be, because my friend no longer could.

Her death made me feel vulnerable. Parents teach their children to avoid dangers they can see, but no one can see into the hearts of men. No one could have predicted that a casual hello would forever alter Laura's life course. Her death made me cautious and, in doing so, took away another part of my inno-cence. I learned that sometimes bad things happen to good people. This situation impressed upon me a need to be cautious and prepared to die at a moment's notice. It also showed me that my time on this earth is limited. That if I have things I want to get done, then I must hurry before I too am taken away.

"Vanessa, I'm confused. At times you've talked about death and sounded very matter of fact about it. You've said that you were a mistake and that the thought of dying wasn't something you were scared of. On the one hand, you distance yourself from death because until recently you didn't realize how your passing would affect other people. But when you speak about other people dying, you have always had a great deal of sensitivity about the impact of the loss of their life to the world, their family, and friends. Why is that?"

There are many things that I want to say and none of them I feel I *can* say. I mean, how do you tell someone that his life is worth more than your own?

I know I can't just sit here, so I have to pretend like I'm thinking. Look around the room . . . play with a hangnail . . . stalling . . . stalling . . .

"Vanessa, I'm waiting."

Where do I start? If I say what I want to say, you're going to think I'm crazy. Not that you probably don't think that anyway, but this will be the clincher for sure.

"Try me."

This is going to sound weird.

"To whom?"

To you . . . to me . . . to everyone.

Okay, here goes.

I know I'm going to die.

She waits. The eyebrows go up and it's like she's holding her breath.

No, I mean soon. Call it intuition or whatever you want, but I have always known I was going to die young. There are certain things that I think people know inside them, and for me, it was two things: one, I was never going to get married; and two, I was going to die young.

"But you did get married."

But maybe I wasn't supposed to! I mean, think about it. I was never supposed to move to Texas. My mother and brothers had already packed the moving van. I'd been accepted to an in-state university and made arrangements to live with a family in my church. It was *never* part of the plan for me to move here.

"So, why did you?"

A voice inside me told me I had to. It's indescribable. It's like I've always had this little Jiminy Cricket voice inside my head that's just sort of guided me through life. It's not a schizophrenic thing at all, but if I were to tell people, "Yeah, this voice told me," I'd be hauled off in a minute. I was getting ready to graduate from high school and was having my wisdom teeth out. I don't know if it was the drugs or what, but as I was sitting there in the chair and the surgeon was asking me what I was going to do after I graduated, this voice in my head says, *"You have to go with them! You have to move."* It was so clear and certain. I didn't think it was something I could deny and so I moved with my family. A year later I met my husband. And the funny thing is, I didn't hear that voice again until the night of our first date, and the second I saw him at my front door, this voice said, *"This is the man you're going to marry,"* and I did. But this same voice has also always let me know that I wasn't like everyone else in the world . . . that I don't have as much time to do the things I want to do . . . that I need to hurry up because my hourglass is running down faster than everyone else's.

"Is this the same voice that tells you when to cut?"

No. This voice is like another part of myself. There is an insecure part of Vanessa and that is the voice that tells me to cut. This commanding voice is very nurturing and trustworthy. It never says anything but positive and encouraging things and I feel like it guides me in some of the decisions I make. This is the Vanessa that I want to be 100 percent of the time. I feel like if I had listened to this voice instead of the other ones, I'd feel better about myself and my abilities. But that's where this war of words comes in. On the one hand, I want to listen to the nurturing voice, but then the insecure voice tells me what it says is a lie. Then my dad's voice will come in and reiterate that sentiment that I am a disappointment, so how could I really be the person the positive voice tells me I am. It's very tiresome. Because the negative voices are louder and usually make more sense, I give them the power.

"Are the negative voices the ones that say you are going to die?"

No. That feeling has been something within me long before there were any voices. I think there are just some things you know, and for me, this is one of them. I've always known I was going to be a teacher and I've always known I was going to die early.

"And how have you handled that? Are you scared?"

No. I'm resigned. It's funny . . . I'm a voracious reader, and as a child, I would always read the last page of the book first in case I died before I reached the end. I never wanted to wonder "who did it" in the afterlife, if there is one. And as a college student, I was always double-timing things. No student activities for me, not one football game or dance. I didn't have the time. I had to hurry, hurry, hurry and get it all in before it was too late. I knew I had great things to offer the world but the world wouldn't have me for long, so I had to cram in as many things as I could while I was here.

"Do you think this has anything to do with the cutting?"

Why would you say that?

"Well, when you cut, you're in control of the pain. Do you think you try to control other parts of your life like that too? Anorexia and self-injury are conditions rooted in control. And yet no one can control his or her own death. Is that what you're trying to do?"

No. Any control I have is that which I have taken out of the hands of others. I never want to feel like my life has been a waste, and so I try to use each and every moment of it I can, while I can.

There are so many things I want to do and see before I die and it seems like I can't fit it all in. I get frustrated because it's like the world doesn't realize what time pressure I'm under. Really. People used to say, "Oh, you're so young, you have your whole life in front of you." And I've always wanted to slap them and scream, "No, I don't!"

"So, is this why you're pushing this thing with your dad, because you think you won't have time later on?"

Maybe so; I don't know. I've always been raised to believe that you never want to have any unfinished business when you die. And he is, for me, the greatest source of unfinished business in my life.

"So, what do you want to say to him?"

I don't know. It scares me shitless to think I'm actually thinking of doing this. What if he doesn't want anything to do with me? What if his leaving was the way he wanted me to remember him? What if I am honest with him about all my feelings and he turns things around and makes me feel like the bad guy again? How can I hope to get to the bottom of all these feelings if I don't even know what they mean?

"Do you expect him to apologize to you?"

No.

Don't lie!

Silence.

A faint yes.

Too much to hope for. Be realistic!

Maybe.

That's better. Keep the door to rejection open.

I don't know. I mean that would be asking a lot, wouldn't it? To get an apology from someone who has never apologized for anything in his entire life? But you know what is really pathetic?

I reach for a tissue.

I should be surprised by the tears, but I'm not. It seems like whenever the topic of my father comes up, the waterworks start.

I can't believe after all these years I'm still crying over him! But part of me wants him to apologize anyway. There's a first for everything, right? Sometimes I have this fantasy of me being able to stand up for myself and telling him everything I've always wanted to say but never could. And I imagine him listening—I mean *really* listening—not that half-ass, nod your head like you understand but really you're just placating the person and waiting for them to finish so you can go on doing whatever it is—and then waiting. That's it, just waiting for all the initial shock and fear and anger and sadness to fade away and then saying he's sorry. But not a generic sorry. A *real* sorry. A specific sorry. Sorry for calling me names. Sorry for saying some of the things that he did. Sorry for hitting me and never having the patience to explain why or to show me he still loved me afterward. Sorry that he wasn't strong enough to show me what a real man is supposed to do and be. Sorry that he was never there to send me off on a date—to make sure that the boys in my life were gentlemen and worth my attention and favor. Sorry for leaving me to do *his* job after he left because my mother never could. Sorry for believing that his world was better without me in it!

"How does that make you feel to know you may never get that?"

Disappointed.

Sad.

But not in him.

In myself.

It says a lot about me to need him to say those things to me, wouldn't you say?

"I think you're looking to him for closure when he's not even part of the equation."

I agree. But here's what I know. As a child I was held accountable for *everything*, especially as the oldest child! I think part of me wants *him* to be accountable for his actions, too. His leaving *totally* destroyed my family. I know that sounds dramatic, but it's true. I don't think he realizes that. When he left, my entire world, and that of my mother and brothers, literally imploded. It was like being dropped off on an alien planet. I have *never* experienced anything so painful in all of my life—so gut-wrenchingly, heart-ripping-out-of-my-chest awful. Period. And I think a good part of that pain stemmed from the fact that I was totally unprepared for it. I never saw it coming. I feel like a good part of who Vanessa is died on the day he walked out the door.

"Okay. So let's say you do talk to him. If you could ask him only one thing, what would you ask?"

I think she is expecting some hesitation from me, but there is none.

The tissue has come to pieces in my hand and falls like snowflakes onto my lap. For a split second I think of a snowfield: white, pure, unmarred by human imprint. How I long for that purity. But it will never be. There are too many impressions on my spirit and many of them negative. In another second, I envision an oil slick: birds and sea creatures gasping for air against a foreign agent thrust upon them. That image fits me better and it becomes clearer in my mind as I proceed.

I want to know why my dad hated me so much . . . why he tried over and over again to break my spirit and will. The same strong spirit that he tried to destroy is the *only* reason I'm still here. I'm a fighter. I have a plan. I have a desire to go further in this life than most people can even conceptualize and I think that scares people. I think it scared my dad. I think he envisioned himself as a father of kids who were *not* like him. But he was wrong. The first baby he held in his hands was *exactly* like him! I don't think he knew how to handle it.

I've lived long enough to know that most people will judge others for qualities they themselves possess. It's like they can see it in others but can't seem to see it in themselves. My dad is like that. I want to think that his parents also tried to break his spirit, and that's why he doesn't have a good relationship with them. Maybe he feels as alone and out of place as I do.

Do I really want to think that I am in any way like the man who has hurt me so badly?

Maybe our "differences" aren't really differences at all.

"**All right, ladies.** Tonight we're going to talk about intimacy."

A sea of groans and eyeball rolling.

I shift in my chair and try to will myself into oblivion. If I were really going to die, now would be the perfect time.

"Each of you has constructed an emotional barrier around yourself. For whatever it's worth, each of you believes that who you *really* are isn't as acceptable as who the world wants you to be."

I start to chew on my pen and try to imagine being on vacation. Fresh air . . . scenery . . . friends . . .

For a moment, I allow my mind to wander and I leave my body.

"Vanessa."

Fresh air . . . scenery . . . friends—

"Vanessa!"

Zoom!

Back in my body.

What?

"Are you still with us? Everyone else is writing and you're just sitting there."

Shit! Was there an assignment?

I look around and see the other women writing in their notebooks.

I'm sorry. I blanked for a minute. Can you repeat what you want me to do?

"I want you to write down your feelings about intimacy."

Are you serious?

I feel my face start to burn.

How does sex relate to cutting?

"I didn't say anything about sex, although that can be a part of intimacy. No, I'm talking about the interpersonal relationships you have in your life—the distance you create in those relationships so people can't get close to you."

I don't want to do this. If I pretend to get ticked off, maybe she'll let me off the hook and allow me to do something else.

Look, I really don't see the connection here.

All eyes are on me. The others are waiting to see how successful I will be.

"Vanessa. You have a problem with intimacy; you all do. I want you to start trying to make some connections of your own here between your current behaviors and your fears of abandonment."

I don't have any fears.

"Vanessa, everyone has fears but most people are able to overcome those fears in order to move forward in their lives. Each of you has been brought into this group *not* because of your disorders but because of the fears those disorders represent. That's what I want you to see. Once you come to terms with this, you'll be equipped to take your treatment to a higher level."

She is getting too close. I have to shut this down in a hurry.

Listen, this is bullshit, all right? I don't have any fears except the fear that whatever I'm doing here isn't going to work. I'm afraid that I am going to die by my own hands because I am trying to be someone the world is able to love.

"Vanessa. I know what you're doing and it isn't going to work."

I'm not *doing* anything!

"Vanessa, here's where the rubber meets the road. Here's where we start getting to the heart of the matter. The other things were important, but they were like layers to an onion. You needed to peel those away before you could get to the good stuff. *Here* is the good stuff."

You say that talking about sex is the "good stuff"?

"I already clarified that for you. You're stalling."

Look. I've been coming to this group twice a week now for a while and although some things are better, there are still others that are not. I'm not getting it! Just tell me what you want me to write about because I'm not seeing the connection.

"Vanessa, write about whatever you want in relation to the issue of intimacy."

I don't have any issues with that.

"Yes, you do."

No, I don't!

I start to dig under my chair for my purse. Dammit, where are my keys?

A tear falls in my lap.

I brush it away quickly before she can notice.

"What are you so afraid of, Vanessa? Dying alone?"

Not dying, just being, okay? Look, this isn't going anywhere. Ladies, I'm sorry I've screwed up your group, but this isn't working for me.

Another tear.

Not so quick this time.

"Why are you crying, Vanessa?"

I'm not. I'm pissed off. There's a difference.

"Vanessa, you have a fear of letting people get close to you. Admit it."

A red-hot cinder comes to life in my chest.

My teeth clench.

I don't *have* a problem, all right?

"Vanessa, why do you want to leave?"

I want to be alone.

"Why?"

Because this is crap! I don't want to talk about these things! Week after week I come here and pay for the privilege of pouring my heart out in the hopes that I will wake up one day and *not* want to die. Is that what you want to hear?

"Vanessa, get mad, whatever you want, but you have to push through this. You can't grow anymore if you don't!"

Push through what? What do you want to hear? That when I was little and punished I was sent off, cast off from the rest of the family like a leper? That when my dad left not only was I physically alone but emotionally alone? That even as an adult I feel totally disconnected from the world I live in? That the only time I feel "real" is when I'm bleeding because I can see it, smell it, and taste it? That I long for someone to hold me and tell me everything is going to be okay, but I know that if they do so it's a lie because nothing is ever okay? That if I'm alone I can't hurt, but more important, I can't hurt others? Is that what you want to hear? Do I have a fear of intimacy? No, because for me it doesn't exist.

The room starts to close in on me.

I sit back down.

This is ridiculous. I'm married to the most wonderful person and I can't even let him in.

One teardrop.

Then two.

Three.

"Why not, Vanessa?"

A moment of clarity.

She almost had me there.

I laugh.

Someone gives me a tissue and raises her eyebrows.

I think she believes I'm going to snap.

No one is writing now.

I pick my keys up from where I dropped them.

Okay, I've had it. I'll see you next week, okay?

Nothing.

I walk to the door and put my hand on the doorknob.

"Vanessa. I think you keep others at arm's distance so that they don't leave you like your dad did."

I whip around and shoot darts out of my eyes.

What . . . did . . . you . . . say?

"You heard me."

Why would you say that?

"I think you know why. Why don't you come back and we can talk about it."

So let me get this straight. You think that because my dad left me almost twenty years ago, I won't allow others into my inner circle in case they decide to leave me, too?

"Yes."

I look out into a sea of faces. Two of the women have gone fetal into their chairs and one has filled her notebook page with doodles.

Now you've done it, Vanessa. Look at how selfish you are, taking away valuable time from the others in the group. Are your issues that special? Do you deserve all of this attention? Leave. No one wants to hear about this anyway!

I long to punch a hole in the wall for a breath of fresh air.

It's not too late. You're so close. Just walk out the door. You don't ever have to come back. Scissors lie on the other side of that door. They're waiting for you. No one can get close to you, because if they did, they would see who you really are and be disappointed.

I turn to sit back down and someone hands me another tissue.

Selfish! Selfish! Selfish!

I cry for ten minutes.

I've lost all sense of where I am. It comes as a surprise to find once the tears stop that I'm still in group. Eyes look at me expectantly. The voices have faded into the background and are replaced with my own voice, which takes on a tone of confession.

When my dad left I was completely caught off guard. I knew my parents were going to get a divorce, but I never, in a million years, thought that meant he would leave and never come back. A part of my innocence died that day, and in its place, a resolve to *never* allow myself to be so vulnerable ever again. Period. If my dad could leave my brothers and me, then surely my husband and friends could leave me, too. It was only a matter of time, right? So why wait? Push them away first. Take control of my destiny. I am alone. That's the way it's supposed to be. I don't want to be, but I am. It's the rules.

"But you're not alone, Vanessa. You are surrounded by people who love you and want the best for you."

Yeah, but that's because they don't know who I *really* am. If they find out I'm not perfect, then they will throw me away just like my dad did.

"Do you think your dad threw you away?"

Yes.

The tissue in my hands has disintegrated. It falls from my hands in little papery flakes. I mentally curse it for not being more durable. I have a split-second thought of the perfect invention: a tissue that actually holds up to the emotional crisis you're having.

"Vanessa?"

It's a voice I don't recognize.

It is Sarah, Miss I'll-sleep-with-anyone-for-love.

"My dad threw me away, too."

All eyes are on her now. She rarely spoke, and when she did, it was only because she had been called on.

"I, uh, was raped when I was nine by one of my neighbors. He was older than I was, in high school probably, and asked me to come into his house one day after school. Our mothers played Bingo together on Sundays and he said she had left her markers . . . told me his mother asked him to return them to me."

She draws her knees up under her chin.

I notice she is wearing two different socks. It bothers me.

"And so like a dummy I went in. I mean, he had never been anything but nice before and our mothers were best friends. Why should I have worried about anything?"

The counselor reaches over to hold her hand. Everyone has put pens down and looks at her, fearful of what she is going to say and the ensuing feelings it will resurrect within us.

"But I knew something was wrong when I walked in and he locked the door behind me. I tried to play it safe. I just stood in the hallway and told him I would wait there while he got the markers. My heart was racing and my palms started to sweat but I couldn't move. It's like my feet were glued to the goddamned floor! My mind told me to run, but I just stood there."

Sarah's voice has changed. She sounds like a little girl.

"I must have dropped my backpack because I remember hearing a thud, but then at some point I was on the floor, so maybe that thud was me. I don't know how I wound up on the floor . . . how he . . ."

Her voice, little more than a whisper.

"Anyway, I wanted to die. I tried to hold my breath but I guess he knew what I was doing, because I stopped moving and he slapped me. He said, I like my girls a little more lively, Sarah. Don't just lie there!

"But I didn't know what to do. I hurt . . . and he was so heavy on top of me . . . but I was so afraid and so I didn't *do* anything . . . and just when I thought I was going to suffocate with him on me, it was over. He jumped up and threw a wet dishrag in my face. 'You'd better get going,' he said. 'My mom will be home soon and she doesn't like me to have company when she's not home. Oh, and the markers are by your backpack, okay?' Like I was worried about the markers! I didn't know what to do with the rag. It wasn't enough. I wanted some more. . . . I wanted to just stand in the middle of a car wash and let the soap and brushes rub all of him off of me . . . but . . ."

Sarah's lap is a mound of tissues. Mine, too. I can't look at anyone else— their pain so raw and on the surface now.

I find a hangnail and pull it. Anything to get out of this emotional place. Physical pain is so much easier to deal with. I find another hangnail and pull it too. Nothing. So I squeeze my finger until it turns purple and a red line appears. Finally! My finger starts to pulsate back to life. I stick it in my mouth and try to find the red line with my tongue.

"I . . . ran, that's it. I just ran. I grabbed my backpack, forgetting the markers completely, and ran to my house. I didn't realize until I started undressing that my underwear was gone. He must have cut them off or something because I never remember him pulling them down. And it sounds stupid, but I still remember those underwear because they were my favorites. You know those Hello Kitty underwear that used to have the days of the week on them?

"In the days that followed, I would look at the other day-of-the-week panties in my drawer and think of the Tuesday panties that had literally been ripped from my body. Shortly thereafter I threw the whole set away. I couldn't even look at them without seeing him and feeling him on top of me.

"A few days later, I got really sick. . . . I couldn't pee without it feeling like fire and so my mother took me to the doctor. When he examined me, he realized what had happened, but since there was no way of his knowing *who* had raped me, he asked my mother to step out of the room for a moment. I cried. I sat there and told this stranger everything that happened and he just sat there with his clipboard and penlight like he was taking notes in a college class! No reassuring words, no holding my hands and telling me it would be okay, nothing! It sounds weird but I *desperately* wanted him to tell my mother what I'd said so I wouldn't have to . . . but he didn't. When my mother came back in, he told her I was really stressed and that my body was undergoing changes—that I had a bacterial infection. Can you believe it? I sat there . . . nine years old . . . and told this man I'd been raped and all he can tell my mother is I have a goddamned bacterial infection?"

I can't look at her anymore. To see Sarah's past so clearly makes me feel bad. I secretly ask God to forgive me for calling her Miss I'll-sleep-with-anyone-for-love.

"When my dad found out he automatically assumed the worst. He said, 'The only way a girl your age is going to be getting an infection like that is to be messin' around with them boys. Now Sarah, what have you been doin'? I thought your mother and I had raised you better than that. You lettin' those boys stick their fingers up in you, girl?'"

I feel a hot line of stomach acid rising from my inner core. I am a human volcano and my lava is slowly rising to the surface.

"I didn't know what to say! It never dawned on me that my own father would think that *I* would be the guilty one! I tried to tell him, but the words wouldn't come out. And then these random thoughts . . . my mother's friendship with this boy's mother . . . if I told the truth it would destroy that bond . . . that maybe I had done something to bring this on myself . . . that somehow I was the horrible one and deserved what had happened.

"So I didn't say anything. And he looked at me, shook his head, and walked out of the room. He never hugged or kissed me again. He said that if I wanted that kind of attention to get it from 'them boys' I'd been 'messin' around with.'

"And so Vanessa, I know what it means to be thrown away."

I can't look at her. I don't want to see myself in her eyes. The pain is too much.

"Had my father for *one* moment believed enough in me to realize that I would never just *give* myself away, I probably wouldn't be here. But human beings are meant to be held, you know? And so I ended up doing what he accused me of all those years ago. I was pregnant for the first time when I was twelve. My dad called me a slut and kicked me out of the house. My mother started drinking again. . . .

"And so here I am. I have an issue with abandonment and intimacy, too, but mine has left me with a permanent reminder of just how badly I've wanted to be loved. What have I done to myself? Now who will ever want me? How do you tell another person you love them, but you have an incurable STD?"

I want to ask her if she's ever seen her father again, but it seems rude and impersonal so I don't.

Sarah laughs.

"And you know what the bitch of it is?"

I look at her. I can't believe how quickly she has gone from being so sad to laughing.

"My dad died in the arms of another woman. Yeah. Here the bastard was telling me not to 'mess around with boys' and *he's* the one messing around on my mom. Isn't that rich? I get raped by a neighbor boy and he's fucking around with someone else's mother!"

I swallow. The lava flow has slowly changed course.

I find my voice again.

Did you ever tell him the truth?

"No. My mom came to school one day and told me he had died and that I could move back home if I wanted to. She looked awful . . . had aged twenty years in less than five. And so I did. I moved back in with her and lived there for less than a month before I was raped by one of her boyfriends. I tried to tell her what happened, but she said I was a liar . . . said I would 'always use my body to get my way' . . . was being selfish and 'trying to steal her boyfriend' . . . and so I left. That was two years ago. I swore I would never end up like she is . . . alone and used by men. And look! Here I am! Man, the fruit sure doesn't fall far from the tree, does it?"

She starts crying again.

"Sarah."

A new voice from across the room. Becca.

"I know just how you feel. I was raped, too, by my father . . . for years. And when I grew old enough to fight him off, he left. Said my mother and I were 'too much work.' The only difference between you and me is that my mother knew what was going on and didn't have the courage to confront him about it. She *knew* what he was doing and didn't do *anything!* I've asked her about it, and I think I've realized that her father did that to her and her sisters. In some sick way, I think she believes that's the way fathers show their affection. I don't know. But I know you're not alone, Sarah. Look at us. We're all different, yet once we've started to dig deeper, we are learning we are sort of the same."

She takes a breath and continues.

"Do you think I want to be fat? I mean, look at you guys. Slim and beautiful. And then there's me. People look at me and think I am lazy and unclean because I am fat. But they don't know the truth. The truth is, when I was slim and beautiful, all that boys, *including* my father, wanted from me was sex. And each time I felt them on top of me licking my earlobes or breathing their hot breath on my neck, I died a little. The slim and beautiful Becca is dead. In her place is the 'new' me—fat, cynical, unapproachable, and, therefore, un-rapeable Becca."

Nyla starts to shift in her chair. We all look at her and silently thank her for the distraction.

Becca looks around to see who is listening. We all were.

"And I think you guys are lucky that your dads left. I mean, so they abused you, said some shitty things to you and made you feel bad about yourselves. Who gives a shit? I have to see my old man all the time. Watch him smile at me with a mouth that used to be wrapped over mine . . . look at hands that grabbed my chest before there were breasts to fill them . . . see him slowly turning into a little old man and realizing that the penis that he violated me with is probably also withering away . . . wishing him dead with every breath he takes . . . hoping he chokes on a mouth full of food in my presence so I can watch him grasp for air just like I used to!"

The heat in the room is stifling. Group has never, ever been this honest and personal. It is making me crazy.

I have to say something.

Guys, think about it. We're here, okay? We've won. They didn't get us because we survived, right?

A sea of heads nod.

I look at the therapist.

My eyes are pleading with hers for understanding.

Then you see now why I have to do this; why I must confront my father with these things. I feel like my life depends on it.

As group ended, I wanted to go around and hug everyone but realized that was probably the last thing any of them wanted. We had learned tonight that we were all damaged goods. That like it or not, we were not free from our demons and that when push came to shove, regardless of the image we projected to the world, we were all still little girls on the inside.

I've been thinking a lot about what happened in group and I don't like it.

"Why not?"

The more I think about my cutting and my dad the less of a connection I find. Maybe it's a bad idea for me to contact him. I mean, what could he possibly tell me that I don't already know?

"So, what do you think you should do?"

I don't know. I was so sure last time that contacting him was the right thing to do, but now I'm not so sure. I don't think I can trust him to do what I need him to do. But part of me feels like if I'm not willing to risk, then I won't know for sure one way or the other. Maybe he's changed now. Maybe he would like me better now than he did when I was a kid. Maybe I've done enough things in my life to show him I'm not a disappointment.

The tears start again.

Damn it!

A tissue box finds its way into my peripheral vision.

I have never been so tired of seeing a box in all of my life! I make a mental note to bring a replacement box my next visit. Who knows how many boxes I've used alone!

I take two, then change my mind and pull out two more. I hold one and stick the others underneath my thigh.

But I don't think I can trust him. I mean *really* trust him with this part of me. And you know why I think this?

My voice starts to rise.

Because when I was thirteen years old, I was taken to the doctor to talk about weight and my eating habits. Growing up I saw how my dad talked about fat people. How he seemed repulsed by the fact that they weren't as "disciplined" as he was or whatever the hell he was repulsed by. I heard some of the comments he made to my mother about her being frumpy, and I remember how tired she looked at night after chasing around three kids all day long. You would think her selflessness would have made her more beautiful. I mean, she was tired because she was raising *his* kids! But it was never that way. And so I always knew I would never be fat. My dad could make fun of me for lots of things, but it would *never* be my weight. It never dawned on me that my dad could make fun of me anyway, *regardless* of what I weighed! And so after my mother and I got home from the doctor's office and the words *anorexic tendencies* came up in the conversation, my dad looked at me and called me a "third-world wannabe." Like I wasn't even good enough to have an eating disorder—I just wanted to play around with it a little bit! Can you believe that? I mean, how much plainer could I be? I was in trouble! Here I am, thirteen years old, literally starving for acceptance, and that's his reaction. No understanding. No compassion. Nothing. Just another slap to my self-esteem.

I am hysterical.

And so now the whole idea of me wanting to contact him . . . to put myself in a position to be made fun of, again, is absolute insanity. Why in the world would I want to do that to myself?

"So don't tell him."

My eyes fall to the carpet and then back up to her face.

What?

"Don't tell him. You are in control of what he knows or doesn't know about you. You don't have to tell him anything you don't want him to know."

Okay, fine. Let's say I don't tell him. How is he ever going to know what a big impact he has had on my life? Part of me needs him to know because I want to know if it's possible that someone else in my family has ever been like I am. I can't believe I'd be freakish enough to be the only one to do what I do. I don't think there is a way to find that out without telling him the truth. And besides, what kind of a relationship would that be? I'm sick of the lies. I want the truth, and I guess deep down inside I feel like if I want the truth, then I have to tell the truth.

"Okay. So let's say you tell him and he uses it against you. Calls you weak. Says you can't cope. Tells you to grow up and take responsibility for your own actions. Says the past is the past and to get over it. Then what?"

Then I'm done. Then I guess I'll know the light at the end of the tunnel was a train after all.

"What will you say?"

I don't think there will be anything to say.

And I guess a part of me really will be dead inside. That part of my soul that I have protected, hurt, and nursed back to health will have its lifeline, once and for all, severed.

"I think you need to think about this a little more before you do anything. You need to be 100 percent sure that you are going to be fine with whatever happens. If your dad rejects you, again, then you have to be in a mental place to be okay with that. You can't put your own happiness into the hands of others. If you contact your dad, share yourself with him, and are rejected, then I need to know you're going to be strong enough not to harm yourself after the fact. I don't think you're there yet."

But what if I'm never there?

"Then contacting him has to wait. Think about how you deal with people rejecting you, or what you have done when you feel like you've been a disappointment to someone."

My eyes fall on a six-inch white line down my thigh peeking out from the hem of my shorts. Once bright red, over time it has faded to a barely perceptible white. A faint reminder of my first head-to-head with a razor blade.

———

During my sophomore year of college, I lived in the dormitories. My future husband's dorm shared a common lobby with my own. After having a commuter relationship for a year, we relished the fact that we were only an elevator ride away from one another. I took solace in the fact that more often than not, when I was studying, he was doing the same thing at a desk, exactly like my own, just a few yards away.

I don't remember the occasion, but I remember I had something special that I wanted us to do. I had worked nights all week so that I could get this particular weekend off. I had things all planned out. The only part of the equation I had missed was to let my boyfriend know about my special plans. This was my fault, although I wouldn't acknowledge it at the time. For many months we had spent every weekend together. I assumed this weekend would be no different. He, not knowing of my plans, made other arrangements with one of his study groups. In hindsight it was no big deal. But at the time, I felt slighted. I felt like I had sacrificed my time and energy for something that had been dismissed, totally unappreciated. "You don't mind, do you, Vanessa? I know we were supposed to spend this weekend together, but I really have to study. I'll call you, okay? Maybe we can meet later in the dining hall for dinner." There was a quick moment of hesitation, then a nodding smile of understanding, and he was gone. Whisked away by matters more important than me. I was fuming. By the time I rode up the elevator to my room I could barely see through the tears. I hated the fact that he hadn't asked me to help him study, and I hated myself for being fool enough to make big plans without telling him about them first.

I don't know how much time passed before I looked out the window and realized the sun had gone down. The clock showed the dinner-serving hours were almost over and my phone hadn't rung. I knew if I called him on the phone he'd answer. But I didn't want to be the one to interrupt him. I didn't want to appear needy, and so I didn't call. My tears had dried into white, crusty streaks down my cheeks and my trash can overflowed with shredded tissue fibers. I decided to take a shower and go to bed. I grabbed my towel and showering kit.

At some point in my shower I decided to shave my legs. I was still angry and tried to come up with something carefree and witty to say if my phone rang later that evening. I remember lathering up my right thigh and uncapping a new disposable razor. I think I had made two sweeps up my thigh when the blade hit a patch of soap and slipped, running on its edge up my thigh. It happened in a second. A long flap of skin hung from the razor blade and my thigh had opened up like a fillet. At first the skin was white, but as soon as the hot water touched it, blood pooled to the surface. To this day I have never bled as much as I did that night. I called out for someone, hoping there might be a person in one of the bathroom stalls. Nothing. I shut off the water and tried to figure out a way to compress my thigh while covering myself as I walked down the hall. As I left the shower room I called out for someone, anyone. Nothing. Everyone either had gone out for the evening or was so far down the hall they couldn't hear me.

I had to keep moving and blood ran down my leg, spotting the floor with every step. "Hello?" Still nothing. "Could somebody help me?" Silence. The walls started to spin. I remember knocking on the resident assistant's door before the darkness swallowed me whole. When I came to, several girls were trying to get me into my bed. "Vanessa, where are your clothes? You need to get stitches." I numbly pointed to random drawers and ended up wearing a mismatched outfit. "Do you want us to call someone?" I desperately wanted them to call my boyfriend across the way but said nothing.

There was a knock at the door. "Vanessa!" It was him! "Vanessa, are you okay? What happened?" He raised the towel from my thigh, grimaced, and replaced it. "We need to get you stitches." "No, I think I'll just lie here for a little while. You need to study. Go on, I'll be okay." "No, I want to make sure you're going to be all right." His worried look made me feel bad. Purposeful or not, I had put it there. "I'm fine, really. The girls will help me. You go on back to your study group."

And so he did. I promised him I would go get stitches—would rest for a while and then have someone take me. But I didn't. I thought of the cost and all the money I didn't have, and so I let it go. Part of me felt like had I gotten stitches it would have attracted more unwanted attention to what I'd done, and so I just let it go. I covered it up, tended to it like I had done all the others, and waited for a scab to form so I could rip it off over and over again until the scar tissue would prevent it.

"You remember a lot about that night."

Yeah. It was one of those turning points for me as a cutter. Before that night I had never been hurt with anything except scissors or blunt instruments. That night showed me the power of the razor blade, and I learned I was strong enough to deal with it.

"So how did your cutting change after that night?"

Part of what made that night so scary for me was that it was accidental. I never intended for it to happen and so when it did, it caught me totally off guard. But it also showed me something I hadn't really considered before: Razor blades cut deeper and therefore give a bigger "rush" than do other instruments.

"But that's a pretty dangerous association to make. Razor blades can kill you."

I know. That's why I keep coming to see you. I have to find out why I even need to cut so that I can stop. I feel like my pain tolerance has built up so much now that I very easily could cut too deep and it would be over. I really am afraid that at some point I am going to get so angry or depressed that I will just sort of leave my body, cut too deeply, and then die. That's not my intention, but I don't know how to avoid it.

"Are you still taking your medication?"

Yes, but I don't think it's working anymore.

"I think you might want to think about talking to your doctor about increasing your dosage."

I laugh. The tissue in my hands has been reduced to white, dandruff-like flakes.

I start picking the minute white fibers out of my sweater.

I was hoping you would let me go off the pills for a while.

"You're joking, right? Vanessa, look at the depth of the issues we're dealing with here. You've never been able to go this far, and I think the medication is part of the reason why. It's balanced you out a little bit. I would be really afraid for you right now if you weren't on them."

Great, so now I have that as a crutch too.

"Vanessa, you don't have to be on these pills forever, but I think right now they're critical. If you were to stop them right now, today, think about the consequences. You don't want your emotions to take over. You're talking about getting to the heart of your behavior, which means we are having to dig deep down inside of you . . . the sad and lonely part of your soul that you've tried desperately to protect for almost twenty years. There is still more work to do and I need you to be balanced. I don't want you to stop taking your pills, come to see me or go to group, and then go home and cut. That's never been my intention. But I think you would be kidding yourself if you were to tell me that you haven't gone home and cut after one of our sessions. Am I right?"

Yes. But cutting isn't working anymore!

I used to be able to cut and get some sort of release out of it. But not anymore! Now it's like I need other things. Hammers. Screwdrivers. Meat tenderizers. I roam the isles of the housewares department in a store looking for something I can use to deal with these feelings! Cutting isn't enough. Now it's like I need to start breaking things.

"Like what?"

I pull up my sweater sleeve.

Like this!

My forearm is black and blue.

"Is it broken?"

I don't think so, I—

"Vanessa, I think we need to talk about you going to a treatment facility. I don't think I'm equipped anymore to deal with your level of behavior."

I stand up and walk to the window. I reach out to touch the glass, hoping there is none and I can fly away . . . anywhere but here.

Do you see what she's trying to do to you, Vanessa? Send you away. You're too much even for a professional to handle. She wants to be rid of you just like your father did. When are you going to get the message?

I can't leave.

"Why not?"

I can't afford it. I have already researched it. The places you're talking about are thousands of dollars. I can't even pay rent, so how in the hell would I pay for something like that?

"Vanessa, I don't know that we have a choice. You're not getting any better. I didn't realize you were beating yourself now, too. What's going on? Why have you not brought this up before?"

I sit on the floor with my head in my hands.

Because I didn't want you to give up on me. I didn't want to be a disappointment to you, too. I want to get better; I really do. But maybe I can't. Maybe I'm beyond help. I knew if I told you about this you would say exactly what you just did and affirm the fact that I am too much . . . that you can't help me, and you would send me away.

"Vanessa, what happened to your arms?"

I hit them.

"With what?"

Whatever I could find: shoes, screwdriver handles . . . anything that I could put my fingers on in a split second. Whatever I could use that I believed would be strong enough to give me that release . . . to give me that resounding "snap" and I would be free.

"Free of what?"

Of all these stupid feelings. Of all this!

I throw my hands up in the air.

I don't want to die and I felt like if I cut any more I might. So I had to find something else. Shoe heels. A hammer. But you know what? I couldn't even do this right!

I pull my sleeve back down.

I was afraid of how out of control I was and so I didn't hit with my full force. It's like I wanted to break my arm, but I wouldn't let myself. It's like there was this internal tug-of-war and one part of myself was saying, "Do it, do it!" and the other was saying, "Are you sure you really want to do this? Do you know what will happen once you cross this line?" and so this is what I ended up with. How pathetic is that?

"Vanessa, I want you to come see me tomorrow."

But I'm not supposed to see you until next week.

"But I want to see you tomorrow. I have an assignment I want you to do for me, and I want us to talk about it tomorrow."

I take off my glasses and start to massage my temples. A headache in the distance runs to the back of my eyeballs, gathers speed, and meets itself in the middle of my forehead.

"Do you have photo albums at home?"

Sure. You mean of prom and stuff?

"No. Younger than that. Childhood photos, photos that were taken about the time when your dad left."

A few.

"Good. I want you to dig those out and spend some time looking at them. *Really* looking at them. What are the circumstances of the picture? Who is in the picture? What do you remember about that picture being taken? Look deep into your eyes."

Are you serious? *This* is going to help me quit cutting?

"Bear with me. I want you to look into your eyes. Who is the Vanessa in those pictures? Is she happy? Is she scared? What does she envision her life will be like? What are her greatest fears? Who *are* you in those pictures?

"Vanessa, there was a time when the part of yourself that is hurting now wasn't. I want to see if you can find a picture of yourself at that time. And then I want you to find a picture of yourself after that time, when you are hurting. My question to you is whether there is a difference in your eyes. I want you to look at the eyes; that's very important."

Yeah, the eyes are the window to the soul, right?

"Right. So let's see if we can't find the part of yourself that you say is missing. The part that is buried beneath all this anger and shame. Let's see if we can bring her into the light and love her. She needs you and you need her."

That night I found the pictures I'd been told to look for: school pictures, church camp, birthday parties, Christmas mornings. My entire life reduced to a series of snapshots. And even though I'm supposed to be looking at the pictures, I can't help but wonder about the person taking the pictures. I think of how much of my parents' lives were not captured on film because they were taking pictures of my brothers and I. How, for those moments, we were the most important things on the face of the earth. And I realized, as I turned the pages of the albums, that despite what I'd feared for so long, with all these reminders, I could never disappear.

Hope. That's the difference.

"What do you mean?"

In my eyes. That's the difference between the old Vanessa and the one sitting here. When I was small, my eyes were filled with light, hope, and wonder. It's almost like I knew a secret and was so excited to share it with someone. I was just glowing from the inside.

I scan the office and realize, for the first time, that there is no visible clock.

"So what happened?"

I don't know. It's like life got in the way or something and that inner light died. And it's funny. I thought it was all of a sudden. I thought that there would just be one picture where there was light and then the next day, a new picture, and no light. But that wasn't the case. It was gradual. You can see it. The older I got, the dimmer the light. The more serious my expressions. In fact, there are some pictures where I'm not smiling at all. I'm just staring at the camera and you can tell I'm dying inside.

"So what did that show you about yourself?"

That there isn't a quick fix. I didn't get this way overnight and nothing I can do will act like a switch and turn off my urges to cut. I have to really work on this and re-create that hope in my life.

She smiles. Her pen creates a rhythm in her hands.

"So how do you think you can do that?"

I have to let some things go.

"Good. Like what?"

Like caring what other people think.

"And what else?"

And believing that just because I fall short of other people's expectations, I am worthless.

"Anything else?"

I have to accept that I will *never*, no matter what I do, be perfect.

"And?"

I can't keep hurting myself. I have to develop a new coping mechanism that isn't so harmful and isolating.

Sniff.

Tears, again. Surely after a certain point I won't be able to cry anymore. But that day isn't today, and so I sit here feeling my eyes weep. My eyeballs feel like they've been rolled in sand. To open them is painful and so I sit with my eyes downcast, half closed.

"Where are the tears coming from, Vanessa?"

I'm afraid. What else could I possibly do that will give me the release that hurting myself does? You're asking me to give up something I've done since childhood. Maybe we can come up with a compromise. Maybe I can still do some things but not other things.

"Do you think that's realistic?"

I run my fingers over the couch. It's new.

Realistic? No, probably not. But it has to be better than going cold turkey and totally failing.

"How many times do you think it takes the average cigarette smoker to quit?"

A lot.

"Yes, a lot. Like more than ten times for some people."

But there are other people who try to quit and never can, regardless of how many times they try.

"True, but you can't assume that's going to be you. You have a powerful spirit. If you want to quit, you will. It may take you some time, but I really think you can beat this thing."

I know you said I wasn't ready to talk to my dad, but I think I have to. I think all of this needs to happen at the same time. If he rejects me or uses what I tell him against me, then I guess I'll have to deal with that. But I can't keep living in fear about his reaction. I have to let this go. I have to feel like I am a complete person and I don't see any other way around it.

"So, do you think it's up to your dad to make you feel that way?"

No. But I think by asserting myself in his eyes, I will be able to put some things to rest.

"Like what?"

When I was little I was powerless. I had to take whatever was thrown my way whether I agreed with it or not. If I stood up for myself, I was slapped. If I exhibited a strong will, it was a source of conflict. I never had a say in anything that happened to me. I feel like I never had a voice. I was never asked for my side of the story. Heck, I don't think my parents ever realized that most of the time there was a story!

"And now?"

Now I can stand up for myself. I have a voice. I am able to articulate my thoughts and feelings in a way I was never able to as a child. I think it will mean a lot to my spirit to be able to look my dad in the eyes and tell him, for the first time in my life, that *I* am disappointed in *him*, that *I* deserved better most of the time, and that my brothers and I are his greatest life's work, *not* his job, and he threw us away.

"How do you think he is going to react?"

I don't know. But what I do know is that I want his voice out of my head. If I screw up, I don't want his voice to be the first I hear. I think if he and I are able to talk about this, that part of himself that is imprinted in me will go away.

"Let's say you do this and he is receptive. Maybe he's sorry and at a place in his life when he can openly talk to you about this. Is there anything he could say that would make you stop hurting yourself?"

I don't know.

"I think you need to figure that out. If you are looking for something specific, you need to know what that is so you will recognize it when you see it. If you are leaving this cure to chance, then you have to accept that you may have to take whatever you get."

———————

Dad,

Good afternoon. It has been many years since we've seen each other and I think it's time. I've thought long and hard about the best way to contact you, and I suppose, in this case, a direct approach is best. I've been advised not to contact you, but I felt strongly that I should. In your last letter, you said that when the time was right, you and I could sit down and talk. You said you wanted to answer my questions and I've tried to figure out a way that my questions might be answered. I am hesitant to even make this attempt, as part of me feels that if you were truly interested in what has happened in my life, you would have made the first move. But the older I get, the more I understand about legal issues in cases like this, and perhaps you were advised not to try to find me. In any case, I think it is time that we lay down our swords and put hurt feelings aside. I know you have a side of the story and I'm curious to know what that is.

I really only have one question, and I wanted to give you time to think about it so you could answer it completely. The thing I most want to know, in spite of all that has happened over the last eighteen years, is when did you know you didn't want a family anymore? I have looked through the picture albums and have been told how badly you wanted each of us children. How, in the beginning, you were so proud to be a father. Was it too much? Was it your career? When did you know you'd made a mistake? Was it something that built up over time, or did something happen to force your hand? I have a theory—all of your children do.

We are standing at a fork in the road. I have two choices: I can send this e-mail or I can delete it. Both paths will lead to different ends. You also have a choice. You can pretend you never received this, or you can read it and respond. I am fine with either choice.

Regardless, I hope this finds you in good health and high spirits. It sounds like you are doing well and I am glad. I, too, am doing very well.

Life is too short to harbor hard feelings.

Vanessa

The office is cool when I go in. I pull my sweater tighter around me. As I sit down I notice my thighs—smaller, but still touching. I make a mental note to work on that. But where to find the energy?

"So where is your mother in all of this? You talk a lot about dealing with your feelings with your dad, but I imagine you also have some unresolved issues with your mother."

Overall my mother has been my greatest cheerleader. She was the one to go to all my school concerts, parent/teacher meetings, and award ceremonies. If I was sick at school, she would be the one who came to pick me up. If I was upset over something someone had said, she would be the one to come in and talk to me about it. But overall, I think I'm a tremendous disappointment to her.

"Why do you think that?"

Because my mother wanted a daughter whom she could teach things to. How to quilt. How to cook things from scratch. How to raise children of my own. And I haven't been interested in any of those things, and so I think that she feels, as a result, that I'm not interested in her.

"And are you?"

Of course! But we're on two different pages most of the time. When I was small, my parents spent a great deal of money on this life-size baby doll for me. She had a high chair and clothes and plastic feeding utensils—everything a kid would want who was going to play with dolls. But not me. I was more interested in the box she came in! My mother begged me to play with "Pink Baby." When my younger brother was born, she would tell me to go get my baby so we could hold our babies together. I wanted none of it. If I had dolls or stuffed animals, they were my students, not my children. I saw how hard my mother worked to be a mother and I didn't want a life like that. I didn't believe I was capable of being as patient and understanding and loving as she was toward us, so I just shut off that part of my personality. My mother wanted to show me "mother" things, but I was more interested in being like my father, a teacher.

"Do you think this has damaged your relationship with her?"

I glance around the office again and look for a clock. I still don't find one. Whereas it had been cool when I walked in moments ago, the temperature in the room seems to have risen 10 degrees. I start to unbutton my sweater.

I look into my therapist's eyes.

I don't think my mother realizes how much I love her. I think she believes that I think that what she has done with her life isn't important, but that's not true. I think my mother feels ripped off because the only girl in her life wants none of the knowledge she has to give. One of the greatest gifts I could have given my mother was children of my own. She has wanted to be a grandmother for as long as I can remember, and I can't do that for her and it makes me sad. It makes me sad because I know that many of the skills she has like quilting and canning and sewing will die with her. I haven't been able to use any of it. But it doesn't mean she hasn't given me skills. I just think she feels like she had so much more to give me and I rejected it.

"Have you told her this?"

In my own way. As an adult I have tried to share as much of my life and life experiences with her as I could. If I was going somewhere and she could go, I invited her. If I was doing something interesting, I invited her to do it along with me. I want to think that I have enriched my mother's life in lots of ways. Unfortunately, it has been in ways neither of us could have predicted.

"It sounds like you feel you're a disappointment to both of your parents. You say your dad threw you away and your mother can't relate to you or the things you value. Is that right?"

I find a loose thread on my sweater and pull. A baby blue button lands in my lap. I finger it and run my thumb over the now empty holes on its face.

You know what I want? I want to die happy. I want to die knowing that both of my parents love me and appreciate how hard I have worked to make them proud. I want to believe that the best parts of each of them flow in my veins. But I think I'm starting to see what has been happening. Just because I exhibit certain character traits doesn't mean I will turn out just like that person.

"What do you mean by that?"

She leans forward, resting her elbows on her knees. I can't look at her. I am going into a place I haven't been in a long time and it scares me. I regret having unbuttoned my sweater and think of asking her to turn up the heat.

When I was small, I could see how my parents interacted. My dad was boss. Whatever he said, went, regardless of whether it was right or wrong. I saw how many times my mother would just sit there, lips pursed, vein bulging out of the side of her head, powerless. I can remember so many times thinking, "Why don't you say something?" and she wouldn't. She would just sit there, fuming in silence. I vowed *never* to be powerless, and so the part of me that was like my mother I repressed. I confused her sensitivity with weakness, when in reality, she just wanted peace in the house. She knew that standing up to my dad would have been more trouble than it was worth, and so more often than not, she bit her tongue just to avoid conflict. I didn't realize it then, but I do now. My mother valued harmony over having her way. I guess that's one major difference between us. I would rather voice my opinion and stand up for what I think than to have peace. I believe that true peace can only be reached after both sides have been heard and understood.

And so as a child, I developed a strong resolve. I read books with strong female characters in them, and I modeled my behavior after them. I didn't realize until later in life that there were other parts to the story that never appeared in any of the books I'd read—like how difficult their lives were compared to their submissive cohorts. How these were women before their time and they were socially ostracized for it. How these strong women would have been the same ones to be accused of witchcraft and never be taken as brides. But at the time I thought that was the better way, and so I was the reason, most of the time, for there being times of unrest in the house. I wanted to stand up and assert myself because my mother didn't think that she could. And that led to a battle of wills most of the time. I imagine now that I got my mother into trouble with my dad sometimes over my stubbornness and her inability to control it. I feel bad about that.

The button has slipped from my hands and bounced onto the carpet. I glance down to find it and can't. I feel naked and vulnerable.

I find another string and start to twist it between my fingers.

And so over the years, I started to develop those parts of myself that were like him—the discipline, the attitude, the drive—because I thought his was the better way. But after he left the family, we were all so angry. Especially me! Here I had spent all of this time and energy to be just like him, and he walks away! I wanted to distance myself from the person I was most like by shutting down those parts of myself that were like him. I didn't want to add insult to injury by being a constant reminder of my father to my mother with my behaviors, and so I hid them. I told myself these characteristics were bad because of all the pain they brought to other people. I didn't want to be like that, but I was. I think part of me believed if I "killed" that part of myself, I could evolve into someone else, someone better, someone more acceptable.

"Is that why you feel like you don't know who you are?"

I look up and find the button on the floor. It has landed near the planter and so I reach down to pick it up.

A small baby blue item of comfort. I run my fingers along the holes again, careful not to drop it a second time.

That has to be it. I think I've always thought that if I were more like my mother I would be weak, powerless, and end up married to a man whom I hated. But if I were more like my father, everyone would think I was an asshole and hate me. I didn't want to be either of those things, so I've tried to figure out a way to destroy those parts of myself that I believed were negative.

"But you can't go against your nature, Vanessa. You are who you are. And you're supposed to be like your parents. Their characteristics are all over your DNA. No amount of cutting is going to get rid of those things."

But I think that's what I've been trying to do. Don't you see? I think, in some small way, I believed that I could do just that. Think about your blood. When you lose some, you make more, new blood. If you skin your knees, new skin grows in its place. I really think that's what I've been trying to do—get deep enough into the heart of who I am so I can cut out the bad parts and new, better parts would grow in their place. Then and only then would I be the new Vanessa. The improved Vanessa. The *best* Vanessa.

"Why do you think you need to be improved?"

I stare at the button in my palm. So small and blue. Chipped on one side. I wonder why I haven't noticed that before.

Have you ever read a book called *The Blessing*? It is based on this Bible story about two brothers. The father is old and dying. One day, while the father is sleeping, the mother dresses the youngest son in furs and sends him in to get his father's blessing. The father, tricked by the furs into thinking he's speaking to his eldest son, grants the young boy his blessing. Later, the eldest son comes in and asks for his father's blessing and the father tells him he had only one blessing to give and he'd already given it away. That's what I feel like. I feel like when I was supposed to get my blessing, there was no one there to give it to me. Your parents are the ones who are supposed to validate *who* you are, to tell you that you're fearfully and wonderfully made, and to say that they are proud of you and the person you've become. But there was no one there to do that and so I thought I wasn't any of those things. My dad was gone and my mother was so spent just trying to survive and take care of my brothers that I was left to draw my own conclusions.

"And how did you draw the conclusion that you weren't a good person?"

Do we really have to talk about this now?

"Why not?"

Because I'm not ready. The other stuff was okay, but I'm not comfortable with this.

"I want you to keep going, Vanessa. What made you think you weren't a good person?"

I feel a wall of water rising up in the corners of my eyes and I close them to dam the flow. My nose starts to run.

BECAUSE I FEEL LIKE HAD I BEEN A BETTER PERSON . . . HAD I BEEN THE CHILD THAT THEY WANTED, THEY *NEVER* WOULD HAVE GOTTEN A DIVORCE!

There, I said it.

As the oldest child, I was always asked to be the big helper, to do those little extra things that parents need their kids to do to make their lives easier. I was the problem-solver child. I was the fixer. If there was a problem, I *really* believed that I had enough good ideas to solve it. But I couldn't fix this. The most important problem of my life and none of my ideas were the right ideas. My dad leaving proved that. Poof! Gone! Had I been enough of a helper and wonderful enough, he never would have been able to stay away. And my mother? Her life was forever changed when my dad left. She had counted on me so much to help her before, but when it really counted, I couldn't! What if it was *my* fault? What if *I* was the reason he threw us all away. He told me that I was a disappointment, that I was retarded, that he wanted me out of his sight. If I was such a failure as the oldest child, what possible hope could he have seen for the younger kids? I hated myself for not being strong enough to just run away! To give him his wish so he could have been happy. I feel like the whole family has suffered because of me and my not being able to be the person they needed me to be.

I can't stop crying.

But I'm trying to be! I'm trying to make him proud of me. I don't want him to think I'm a disappointment forever! One day I'll be famous enough for him to find out about some of the things I've done in my life and he'll realize what he has missed out on. But I will still have failed because it will be *too late.* The family doesn't need him anymore. When we needed him the most, he wasn't there. And as the oldest child, I feel like I carry a part of the blame for that. Had I been perfect, there is no way he could have left and our family would still be together.

I want to throw up.

I feel like I'm thirteen again.

"So is that what you want? Him to come back?"

No! That's what is so stupid about this whole thing! I don't need him anymore! When I did, he wasn't there! How could I *not* think I was worthless when my own father just walked out the door and never came back? Do you think he has any idea of how devastating that was? No one wants to feel like their parent hates them, but I do. I feel like my father wanted a good, obedient child. Instead, he got a strong-willed, purpose-filled child. He wanted someone who could live up to his expectations, but I *never* could. He wanted someone who wasn't a continual disappointment, but that's not what he got.

A pile of tissues has appeared on the side of the couch. I don't remember taking any, or using any, for that matter.

You know what he got?

The counselor looks down at her hands. She reaches out for mine, but I pull away.

You know what he got?

Me! That's it! *Me!* And no matter how hard I've tried to be something different, I'm not! *I'm still me!*

I stand up and walk to the window. Such a beautiful day outside and such a dark day inside. I feel like a caged animal at the zoo.

I turn and look at my counselor.

I think I thought if I cut out all the bad parts I would be better . . . loveable.

"And what are those bad parts, Vanessa?"

The fear. The anger. The strong will. All those things that make me difficult to live with.

"And what did you expect to grow back in their place?"

Patience. A stronger but more focused drive . . . more discipline . . . and . . .

I turn back toward the window.

"Perfection?"

I walk back to the couch and collapse. Defeated. Exhausted. And then from deep within comes a small, quiet voice.

Yes. Perfection.

———————

Dear Vanessa,

It was so good to hear from you. I would love to meet with you at any time and place of your choosing. Distance is not an issue. I will fly out to meet you wherever you are; you just let me know about a convenient day and time. Look so forward to hearing from you.

Dad

"**Ladies, as you know,** we are down to our last group session. I think each of you would agree that you have come a long way over these last few months."

A sea of heads nodding in unison.

"I want you to take a moment and look through your notebooks. Look at some of the things you wrote about when we met: anger, forgiveness, acceptance. Each of these aspects represents a part of you and is connected in some way to your behavior. We've examined each of them carefully in private and group sessions, but now I want you to step back and see if you have found greater understanding of yourself once you put all these issues back into one framework."

No one moves.

I look around to see whose eyes I can meet. Believe it or not, I feel sad inside.

"Why is no one doing anything?"

Nyla, for the first time ever in group, speaks without hesitation.

"I can't believe this is the end. I don't think I'm ready yet."

"Nyla, this isn't the end. This is the beginning. I *know* this is scary."

A laugh.

"Remember how afraid everyone was just to be *in* a group? No one wanted to talk about the parts of themselves that now you are more comfortable with. The whole purpose of this group was to give you some tools for understanding yourself better and you have those now. Does that mean everyone in here is fixed or has her problems solved? No. But are you farther along down the road than you were months ago? Absolutely. Group is meant to be a short and intensive process. Some of you may feel like you could still benefit from participating in another group and we can talk about that individually. But overall, you guys have done exactly what I wanted you to do and that was to move closer to a better understanding and to forgive yourselves."

I reach under my chair for my notebook. Once perfectly flat, it looks now almost weather-beaten. Wrinkled pages from teardrops. Bent edges and a ridge of white paper. A testament to the pages that served as a confessional to my deepest and darkest fears and then were sacrificed for them.

Slowly, one by one, the sound of pages turning. Some fast. Some slow.

I start to read what I wrote on the first day of group and then casually flip through to some of the other pages. I am overwhelmed by the honesty on these pages. Events and thoughts I had sworn to never tell a soul are staring back at me in multicolored splendor. For a fleeting moment I consider ripping all the pages out, hiding any evidence of the shame I've carried with me for so long. But I can't. My notebook seems almost sacred to me and I close it and hold it to my chest.

I shut my eyes and listen to the other women as they breathe, turn their pages, and move in their chairs. How often I have sat in this chair and imagined myself somewhere else.

But not tonight.

Tonight, I want to absorb all that is going on around me. I want to imprint it on my soul so that I might never forget it. This closet, this poor excuse for a therapy room, and a group of women who I swore I had nothing in common with, have changed me. I sit now and relish the change.

"As we look to the end of our group, I want you to take some time to think about what I asked you to do. In the beginning, we took a large issue and broke it down into smaller pieces so that each of you could see the relevance of those pieces. Now that you have greater understanding of those pieces, I want you to put them back together into a larger whole and write about what you make of it now. How has your understanding of yourself changed through group?"

I flip to the end of my notebook and find a clean, white page—one of the few totally smooth pages of the notebook. This page is unsoiled with tears and I run my fingers over the surface of the page. Part of me longs to sniff it, but I smile to myself instead and start to write.

When I started group, I imagined my life to be a runaway train driven by a mad conductor. This conductor cared nothing about me and did whatever he could to see that I was miserable. I wasn't able to steer it or control the speed of the train. I had no say over who was on the train with me, but I felt compelled to make each of them, whether I knew them or not, like me. I believed that I had two choices. One, I could stay on the train that I believed would one day veer off a cliff and kill me, because I was a failure for not being able to please everyone or gain control over the train. Or two, I could try to wrestle control of the train away from the conductor. The problem was the conductor was my past and I was more fearful of it than I was the train falling off the cliff. And so I did things to cope—to make this horrible train ride tolerable. Unfortunately, the things I was doing to cope were more destructive than anything the conductor could come up with. In the end, I resolved myself to dying. But I wasn't afraid of dying because I wasn't sure I deserved anything better.

But now, I think life is more like a seismograph, that there is some cosmic needle recording the events of my life. For better or for worse. Every day. A little peak when I find money in the pocket of my jeans. A little dip when I go to the grocery store and buy everything except the thing I went there for in the first place. A huge peak when I get a new job. A huge dip when I lose it. And I think that's the way it should be, so that at the end of my life, God will hand me this ticker tape and all of my highs and lows will be recorded there. Most of them I will have forgotten, but they will be there, labeled, for me to go back to and revisit. I think of how many times in my life I have prayed for things to happen. To get an A on a test. To find an outfit "I just can't live without" in my size. To find a parking space close to the door when it's pouring down rain. And I think too of how quickly I forget about those things once they happen. And then other things happen in my life and I can never forget them. Stepping on a nail. My first kiss. My parents' divorce. But I'd like to think that there's a record being kept somewhere of all these things, big and small. And it's in this record that the essence of who I really am is. Maybe I don't have to change the world to be remembered. Maybe just by changing my world, I will have done enough. And maybe, just maybe, as long as my friends and family remember me, then I will never disappear.

"I see that most of you have finished writing in your notebooks. Is there someone who wants to share what they wrote?"

For the first time in group, I don't have to be called on to talk. I meet the counselor's eyes and nod.

Walking into the counselor's office *I feel giddy, like a huge burden has been lifted off my shoulders. Had I been alone, I would have done a jump for joy.*

"So, you have decided to have dinner with your father in a couple weeks."

Yes.

"Are you nervous about that?"

Terrified. But it's something I need to do.

"What will you talk about?"

Safe subjects this time. My job. The weather. Books I've enjoyed. I have no intention of sharing with him any of the things we've talked about so far.

"Why not? Isn't that the whole purpose of your meeting?"

In due time. I have to feel the waters out a little bit. You were right. To bare my soul for him at this point would be a huge mistake. I have to make sure that he is sincere in wanting a relationship with me. If he is, then he will be willing to do a lot more than just "fly up and have dinner with me sometime." He has to prove to me that he's willing to see this thing through.

"I think that's a good idea. I'm glad that you are going into this with a game plan and a realistic understanding that he may or may not be serious about having you in his life. It may take months, even years, to determine just what his intentions are and how much of the truth he's going to be able to handle."

You know how long and hard I've wrestled with this. I had to be sure that I was ready and that he was willing. But I know that just because we are meeting once doesn't mean we will ever meet again. And you know what? I'm okay with that. If we meet and it's a complete disaster, then I haven't lost anything. But if we meet and it seems to be going well, then perhaps he will express an interest in meeting again. But I'm not going to push it.

"What happens if he takes one look at you and it's clear you aren't what he expected?"

Then I guess that will have to be something I deal with. It's been a long time. I doubt he's what I'll be expecting either. But I'm not looking to impress him anymore. I know you won't believe this, but I really feel like I am who I am and that's it. I am going to dress nicely and probably prepay for my dinner so I can make a quick escape if I have to, but other than that, what you see is what you get. If this is a ruse for him to see how I've turned out, then at the very least, I will have made the attempt and there can be closure. I just feel like I have to see him one more time, to say the good-bye I never had the chance to say as a child and to show him that my will was stronger than his. I am a survivor and regardless of what he tried to do to my spirit, I'm still here and I think that says a lot.

"I agree. But I don't want you to assume it's going to be a disaster. Go in with some hope of a nice encounter. He may surprise you. Remember, you are a blast from his past. He probably didn't expect to hear from you again. I imagine he's quite nervous about the proposition and has some things he would like you to know about himself as well that he couldn't share with you as a child. Be open to those things. Sometimes answers come when we haven't even asked the questions yet."

It is midnight and the house is quiet. Although my husband is home and relatively close by, I feel completely alone. I pick up the scissors and scrutinize the blade. The steel is cold and unyielding in my palm. The blades have been meticulously cleaned and I set them aside. In the distance I hear the voice.

Go ahead. One more time. What difference does it make? Group is over. No one has to know. Just a little cut. Not much, just a release from all your anxiety. No one could blame you. Go on. You know you want to.

On the countertop next to the scissors is a box of razor blades. Shiny and new, they gleam under the fluorescent tubes. I unwrap one of them and balance it in my hand. It is surprisingly heavy.

The voice again.

Come on, Vanessa. They're here. You're here. Just a little cut. It doesn't have to be deep, but you know how much better you'll feel when you bleed . . . just a little bit. Come on. Hurry! Before anyone wakes up and knocks on the door.

I open the bathroom cabinet and pull out the bottle of alcohol.

Two cotton balls.

One pair of scissors.

I sit on the edge of the bathtub, close my eyes, and breathe.

I take the fingers of my left hand and run them over the scars on my right arm. So many cuts. Triangles. Stripes. Xs.

I think of the situations that put them there.

I open my eyes and walk back over to the countertop. The light over the sink hurts my eyes. But I move in closer so I can see my eyes. Closer, closer, until my nose almost touches the glass.

Who am I? What do I see? Is there hope in my eyes? A glimmer of light?

I lean back and catch a glimpse of my body in the mirror. I reach down and pinch my thighs, my arms, my cheeks.

I feel it.

I'm still here.

I haven't disappeared.

I lean in again to look at my eyes: blue, shining, content.

I find the bottle of alcohol and open it.

I close my eyes and sniff it; then I put the lid back on the bottle and return it under the cabinet.

The voice lurks in the background, more distant than it was just moments ago.

Come on, Vanessa. Just one more time. The last time, I promise.

I pick up the scissors and open them. They feel almost sacred to me as I feel their weight in my hands. I close them and put them back in the drawer.

I close the box of razor blades and set them in the bottom of the trash can. Although new, they seem tainted somehow. I take a wad of toilet paper and cover them up.

The voice again, barely perceptible, gives out one final cry.

Give in to your fears, Vanessa. Your father will reject you. He will see you eat at dinner and think to himself how fat you are. He will kindly listen to all you have to say to him and then bid you farewell after dinner and never look back. He didn't want you then and he doesn't want you now. Go ahead, accept your fate. Use this blade to get rid of the pain. Bleed it away. No one will know. Go on!

And then from somewhere within comes a louder voice: *my* voice.

He may reject me. He may decide he wants nothing to do with me. But I have no control over that. I can only control myself and that's what I am going to do. There may come a time when I am so desperate that I need to cut, but today is not that day.

The razor blade gleams in the light. Its edges are minute and sharp enough to separate the fibers of a piece of string.

But it is not strong enough to make me something I am not.

It is not capable of taking away my feelings.

Its power, at this moment, seems misguided and misplaced.

I wrap the sacrificial lone ranger in tissue paper and put it in the trash can with his comrades.

I look in the mirror again at my eyes. And there, way in the back, is a barely perceptible light. A light that says I have a secret and if I don't tell someone, I'll explode.

It's a flicker of hope.

The darkness started coming for me on Monday.

But it couldn't find me.

Wrapped in an insulation of self-understanding and acceptance, I stand quietly before the mirror, naked. There, I stand and look at myself. My thighs. My stomach. My face. And my arms.

But there are no tears.

There is no shame.

There is only quiet.

I look at the scars and then I look up into my eyes and realize it's okay. It always has been; I just didn't know it.

Epilogue

I wish that I could say that I have never cut again, but that would be untrue. In fact, the reality is that I have gone from cutting four or more times a day to only once or twice a year. It is my hope that as I continue to work to better understand myself, there will come a day when I don't cut at all.

I could have never predicted how healing seeing my father again would be for me. To stand before him, a broken, old man, and assert myself as a well-educated and highly accomplished adult gave me the confidence I needed to explore even more of the issues behind my self-injury. That first meeting was my "aha moment." So many of the images I had in my mind of my father were through a child's eyes and perspective. To see him again through adult eyes validated that he could never physically hurt me again. And I realized, as an adult, that without my allowing him to, he could never again hurt me emotionally either. For the first time ever in his presence, I was in control and that reality was life changing.

As you can imagine, that first dinner together was forced and tedious. Every word we shared was carefully thought out and articulated so as to prevent any misunderstanding. In an effort to prevent vulnerability, our discussion harbored on the inane: work, weather, current events, and movies. But it was a starting point to a new line of communication. At the end of the evening, instead of wondering if my father respected me, I realized his opinion was irrelevant. I respected myself and *that* was most important.

After our initial meeting, my father and I have met once every few months for dinner. These meetings are awkward and forced, but I believe there is value and a benefit to me in my journey of understanding, in spending time with him. The more I spend time with him, the more I realize how alike we really are. Like a crystal ball, my father shows me what I might be like in the future if I don't make more realistic and healthy choices.

An entire year of meetings transpired between my father and I before I shared with him my struggles with self-injury. He asked my brothers and me to spend time with him and his wife over a long weekend at a beach condo in south Texas. I didn't want to go. Not having spent more than an hour at a time with my father in more than twenty years, I believed any long-term exposure to him, and on foreign territory to boot, would be emotionally damaging. But I had to take the chance. I *had* to know that my father no longer held any control over me, and so I went.

In preparation for our time together, I sent my father a list of things I wanted us to discuss. This book was one of them. I told him I needed to talk openly with him about our past and how many of his interactions with me had affected me. He was open to this and encouraged me to bring the manuscript. He promised to read it carefully and to talk to me about it afterward. I knew that by allowing my father to read my words, I was exposing myself in front of him in a way I had never been able to do before and it scared me to death. I can't say what I was most afraid of at the time. Although initially, I feared my father would do two things: deny my memories and laugh about them. It took me two days to summon up the courage to give the manuscript to him. It took him a couple hours to read it. An entire lifetime of pain and confusion, and his response? "Thank you for sharing this with me." That was it.

At first, I thought that my father had been so moved by my words that he needed some time to process them and *then* we would have the conversation I had been promised. Once I got the manuscript back, I looked feverishly for notes from him in the margins—questions, comments, any words his heart felt and his mouth could not say. And there were none. We took a walk alone on the beach and I waited, in silence, for something, anything, from him to acknowledge what I'd shared with him. Nothing. I had already shared so much, I just didn't have the strength to initiate the conversation, and so I waited, trusting he would do it for me. He did not.

Two days later, I had to leave. My heart, my soul, my being, stripped away over time and put together again through therapy and love, was crushed. The discussion I was promised and waited for never happened, and we've never spoken of it since.

I learned something over those four days in south Texas. I learned that I am stronger than my father is for accepting my past and learning from it. I learned that my father's inability to accept any part of his role in my disorders says a great deal about him as a person and where he is emotionally in his life. And most important, I learned that sometimes more can be said in silence than through any words at all. My father did not deny my memories or laugh at them. I'm glad for that.

But I wish that he would have been strong enough to revisit our past once again and help me understand why he is the way he is. That, like many secrets in my family, will die with him.

Do I regret making myself so vulnerable in his eyes? No. I am who I am and he is a part of that. If we are to have any interactions from this day forward, he has to know the *real* me, and this is the real me. Although there remains a hole in my heart, there was healing in this experience. My healing has come *not* from his understanding of the issue, but rather my ability to share it with him.

Like you, I continue to grow. Each day presents its own challenges and fears. But I have learned to openly deal with them instead of hiding behind a stoic wall of false control.

And perhaps one of the greatest things I have learned on this journey is that the only thing I can control is me. It is impossible for me to earn the approval of everyone in my life. I will never have all the answers to questions thrown my way. And at the end of the day, how I feel is up to me. I must celebrate the things I do well and work on the things I don't. I must surround myself with people who like me for who I am, and not for who they want me to be.

And finally, I have learned that the past has only as much power as I give it. It has shaped the person I *am*, but it does not have to dictate the person I will *be!*

May you also find healing as you embrace your true self.

Resources

RESOURCES FOR SELF-INJURY (INFORMATION AND REFERRALS)

National Mental Health Association
2000 N. Beauregard Street, 6th Floor
Alexandria, VA 22311
Telephone: 703-684-7722
Fax: 703-684-5968
Mental Health Resource Center: 800-969-NMHA
TTY Line: 800-433-5959

S.A.F.E. Alternatives® (Self-Abuse Finally Ends)
7115 W. North Avenue, Suite 319
Oak Park, IL 60302
Information Line: 800-DONT CUT (800-366-8288)
Website: www.selfinjury.com

RESOURCES FOR EATING DISORDERS
(INFORMATION AND REFERRALS)

**National Association of Anorexia Nervosa and Associated
  Disorders**
Hotline: 847-831-3438
E-Mail: anad20@aol.com

National Eating Disorder Information Center
Toll-Free: 866-NEDIC-20 (866-633-4220)
E-Mail: nedic@uhn.on.ca

National Eating Disorders Association
603 Stewart Street, Suite 803
Seattle, WA 98101
Business Office: 206-382-3587
Toll-Free Information and Referral Helpline: 800-931-2237
E-Mail: info@NationalEatingDisorders.org

Additional Reading

BOOKS ABOUT CUTTING/SELF-INJURY

Conterio, Karen, and Wendy Lader. *Bodily Harm*. New York: Hyperion, 1998.

Favazza, Armando R. *Bodies Under Siege: Self-Mutilation and Body Modification in Culture and Psychiatry*. Baltimore: Johns Hopkins University Press, 1996.

Kettlewell, Caroline. *Skin Game*. New York: St. Martin's Griffin, 2000.

Levenkron, Steven. *Cutting: Understanding and Overcoming Self-Mutilation*. New York: W.W. Norton & Co., 1998.

Miller, Dusty. *Women Who Hurt Themselves: A Book of Hope and Understanding*. New York: Basic Books, 1994.

Strong, Marilee. *A Bright Red Scream: Self-Mutilation and the Language of Pain*. New York: Penguin Books, 1998.

BOOKS ABOUT ANOREXIA NERVOSA

Hornbacher, Marya. *Wasted: A Memoir of Anorexia and Bulimia*. New York: HarperPerennial, 1998.

Levenkron, Steven. *Treating and Overcoming Anorexia Nervosa*. New York: Warner, 1988.

Smith, Chelsea Browning. *Diary of an Eating Disorder*. Dallas: Taylor Publishing Co., 1998.

About the Author

Vanessa Leigh Vega, M.S., is a high school English teacher and motivational speaker. She is a contributing author to the award-winning *Taste Berries for Teens #4*. She has been nationally recognized for excellence in teaching by being named to the *Who's Who Among America's Teachers* in 2002, 2003, 2004, 2005, and 2006. She has a degree in English/secondary education from Texas Tech University and a degree in health education and promotion from the University of Texas Medical Branch at Galveston. She resides in Irving, Texas, where she is working on her next book. Vanessa speaks about cutting at conferences, schools, and special events. She can be contacted at vanessa@vanessa-vega.com.